D0003145

Contents

Special thanks to my wife and son for their patience and moral support, to my friends for being so forgiving when I was "busy with the book," to Dad for lending me Mom, who provided me with her publishing experience and expertise at the word processor, and to Motorbooks International, a group of the most cordial and helpful people I have ever worked with.

Introduction

I acquired my first car when I was fifteen, and since that time have had more than 100 cars. In the beginning, I was frequently baffled in my restoration efforts because I was unable to locate a part or service needed. Over the years, however, at car shows, by word of mouth or referral, "up front" and "out back," through extensive reading, and trial and error, I have acquired a private directory of sources with which I can do virtually anything. It has occurred to me that my directory would help other car buffs overcome some of the major stumbling blocks in the process of restoring, preserving or building classic or antique automobiles.

The bow-tie is immediately recognized by Chevrolet buffs as the logo for the Chevrolet Division of the General Motors Corporation. This book is an exclusive directory of more than 700 sources for automotive supplies and services available for Chevrolet purists, whether hobbyists or professional restorers. (It might also be noted that many of the sources included here are not exclusive to Chevrolet.)

Let's say you just crunched a fender on your 1941 Chevy. Body panels for this model are no longer available. You need someone to design and build a replacement fender. I have been able to locate only two such people nationwide; both are included within.

Haven't found that special auto yet? Look under "Brokers" in the index. Need a reverberator for a 1966 Impala Super Sport? This listing contains ten nationwide sources. Interested in offering your vintage auto as a prop in a movie? You might want to talk to the

5

people at the Motion Picture Vehicle Owners Club (listing 470).

Need new bows for that vintage convertible? Looking for somebody to do that steering wheel restoration? Need a bumper rechromed? Want your sun visor re-covered? Want new glass? Decals and stencils? Wood graining? Dash pads and overlays? Weatherstripping? Antique or classic tires? Wheel covers? Need an electrical diagram? Looking for a special price or parts book? Need your antique clock or radio repaired? How about rebabbitted connecting rods for a 1927 Chevrolet? In this book you'll find accessories; dry stripping; color-matched aerosol paints; high-performance parts and services; antique auto insurance, appraisals, financing or titles; special hardware and equipment; automobile transport trailers and transportation services; clubs . . . .

The first section of this directory is an alphabetical listing of firms. If you know the name of the firm, but need the address, look in the alphabetical listing. You may also look under the desired category in the index, which contains the listing numbers of firms according to their alphabetical rank. If there isn't a general category for what you need, try "General parts," "Miscellaneous" or "Rebuilding, reconditioning, fabrication or restoration services"; many of the sources in these divisions are either too diversified or too exclusive for a general category. You might also contact any supplier specializing in your particular model (listed in the model categories in the index— "Camaros from 1967 to present," for example); it may be able to provide you with the source you need.

Has your restoration project come to a halt because you don't know where to find that special part or service? It's probably included here.

Good luck on that special project!

Bruce M. Kneifl
Iron Horse Auto

6

Alphabetical listing

1
Adirondack Classic Chevy Club
P.O. Box 691–CBG
Lake Placid, NY 12946

Restoration, preservation and collection.
Any model.

2
AFTCO
P.O. Box 278 HC
Isanti, MN 55040

New, used, new-old-stock, reproduction or rebuilt
    parts and services.
Camaros from 1967 to present.

3
Agape Auto
2825 Selzer
Evansville, IN 47712

Mechanical parts, accessories, body parts, interior
    parts, trim, chrome, electrical parts, hardware
    and other general parts; wheels and wheel
    accessories.
All models, all years.

4
Al Campen
404 12th Street SE
Waseca, MN 56095

Manuals, parts books, price books, catalogs and
    other literature.
Send SASE for catalog.

5
Allan's
8997 River Crescent
Suffolk, VA 23433

Appraisals and estimates.
All models and eras.

6
Allan Tromblay
2955 Quartz Creek Road
Grants Pass, OR 97526

New, used, new-old-stock, reproduction or rebuilt
    body and body trim parts.

7
All Chevrolet Carpet and Trim
310 New Orangeburg Road
Lexington, SC 29072

Interior fabric, hardware and trim.

8
Allen's Exhaust
P.O. Box 736
Logansport, IN 46947

New, new-old-stock or reproduction exhaust parts
    or complete systems.

9
Alliance Cams
3528 Sagunto Street
Santa Ynez, CA 93460

Camshafts ground to original specifications.
Free brochure.

10
A&L Overdrive Sales & Service
7630 West 96th Avenue
Broomfield, CO 80020

New, used, new-old-stock, reproduction or rebuilt
transmissions or parts.

11
American Antique Auto Parts
3612 West Louisiana State Drive
Department C
Kenner, LA 70065

New, used, new-old-stock or reproduction parts and
services.
All 1911-54 models of cars and trucks, excluding
Corvettes.
Catalog, $3.50.

12
American Automotive
3306 North 5th Unit E
Canyon City, CO 81212

Rebuilding, reconditioning, fabrication or
restoration services. Power tops and windows,
power antennae, headlight motors.

13
American Camaro and Firebird Co.
P.O. Box 7175
Boise, ID 83707

New, used, new-old-stock, reproduction or rebuilt
parts and services.
Camaros from 1967 to present.

14
American Classics Restoration
80 Carter Drive
Guilford, CT 06437

Mechanical parts, accessories, body parts, interior
parts, trim, chrome, electrical parts, hardware

9

and other general parts.
All models, all years.
Catalog, $2.00.

15
American Collectors
P.O. Box 8343
385 North Kings Highway
Cherry Hill, NJ 08034

Insurance for antique and restored vehicles.

16
American Corvette
5023 Frank Akins Road
Powder Springs, GA 30073

New, used, new-old-stock, reproduction or rebuilt
parts and services.
Corvettes, all years.

17
American Custom Industries, Inc.
5035 Alexis Road
Sylvania, OH 43560

New, used, new-old-stock, reproduction or rebuilt
fiberglass, body and body trim parts.
Catalog, $2.00.

18
American Hubcap & Wheel Access
931 West Arrow Highway
Glendora, CA 91740

Wheels and wheel accessories.
All models.
Catalog, $1.00.

19
American Speed Equipment
3006 23rd Avenue
Moline, IL 61265

New, used, new-old-stock, reproduction or rebuilt
high-performance parts and services.

10

20

American Stripping Co.
1011 West 45th Street
Norfolk, VA 23508

Dipping and paint stripping.

21

Ames Performance Engineering
Bonney Road
Marlborough, NH 03455

New, used, new-old-stock, reproduction or rebuilt
    parts and services.
Chevelles, El Caminos and Malibus from 1964 to
    present.

22

A&M Soffseal, Inc.
104 B3 May Drive
Harrison, OH 45030

New, new-old-stock, or reproduction weather
    stripping, moldings, gaskets, seals and other
    rubber parts.
Catalog, $3.00.

23

Ancient Cars & Parts
64 North Main
Lyndonville, NY 14098

New, used, new-old-stock or reproduction parts and
    services.
All 1911–57 models of cars and trucks, excluding
    Corvettes.
New, used, new-old-stock, reproduction or rebuilt
    parts and services.
Corvairs and full-sized models (i.e., BelAirs,
    Biscaynes, Caprices, Impalas, station wagons and
    so on), all years.
Mechanical parts, accessories, body parts, interior
    parts, trim, chrome, electrical parts, hardware

and other general parts.
All models, all years.
Catalog, $5.00.

24
Andover Automotive
P.O. Box 3143 HC
Laurel, MD 20708

Interior fabric, hardware and trim.

25
Andover Corvette
P.O. Box 3143 HD
Laurel, MD 20708

New, used, new-old-stock, reproduction or rebuilt
    parts and services.
Corvettes, all years.

26
Anglin Auto
P.O. Box 15023
Hamilton, OH 45015

New, used, new-old-stock, reproduction or rebuilt
    parts and services; interior fabric, hardware and
    trim.
Camaros from 1967 to present.

27
Antique Automotive Engineering, Inc.
3560 Chestnut Place
Denver, CO 80216

New, used, new-old-stock, reproduction or rebuilt
    engines, powerplant parts and so on.

28
Antique Auto Parts
835 Charles Street
Indianapolis, IN 46225

New, used, new-old-stock or reproduction parts and
    services.

12

All 1911–54 models of cars and trucks, excluding
Corvettes.
Mechanical parts, accessories, body parts, interior
parts, trim, chrome, electrical parts, hardware
and other general parts.
All models.

29
Antique Auto Radio
Box 892
Crystal Beach, FL 34681

Sales and repair of new, new-old-stock,
reproduction or rebuilt radios, speakers and
boosters.

30
Apple Hydraulics
610 Nostrand
Uniondale, NY 11553

Shock absorber rebuilding.
Free catalog.

31
ARASCO
Department H86
Box 24
Newport, KY 41072

New, used, new-old-stock, reproduction or rebuilt
body and body trim parts.
Free catalog.

32
Argus Books
P.O. Box 49659
Los Angeles, CA 90049

Manuals, parts books, price books, catalogs and
other literature.

33
Arizona GM Classics
3214 Milber
Tucson, AZ 85714

New, used, new-old-stock, reproduction or rebuilt parts and services.
Camaros from 1967 to present; Chevelles, El Caminos and Malibus from 1964 to present; Monte Carlos from 1970 to present; Novas and Chevy IIs from 1962 to present.

34
ARS Tools & Stereos
Box 1902
Glendora, CA 91740

Sales and repair of new, new-old-stock, reproduction or rebuilt radios, speakers and boosters; special tools and machinery for restoration and preservation.
Catalog, $1.00.

35
Arthur Gould
6 Delores Lane
Fort Salonga, NY 11768

New, used, new-old-stock, reproduction or rebuilt cooling system parts and services; new, new-old-stock, reproduction or rebuilt fuel system parts and services.

36
Artistic Vinyl
453 Saratoga Avenue, Suite 81
Santa Clara, CA 95050

Interior fabric, hardware and trim.

37
ASC&P
P.O. Box 255
Eagle, PA 19480

Rebuilding, reconditioning, fabrication or restoration services.

38

Assurance Appraisal Service
221 Suffolk Avenue
P.O. Box 591
Department H
Revere, MA 02151

Appraisals and estimates.
All models and eras.
Appraisal packet, $4.50.

39

A-TEX Automotive
7606 Sand Building 14
Fort Worth, TX 76118

New, used, new-old-stock or reproduction parts and
    services.
All 1955–57 models, excluding Corvettes.

40

Ausley's Chevelle Parts
7000 Oakley Street
Department SC
Graham, NC 27253

New, used, new-old-stock, reproduction or rebuilt
    parts and services.
Chevelles, El Caminos and Malibus from 1964 to
    present.
Catalog, $2.00.

41

AUTIO FI
4928 Aquatic Road
Department CC
Nashville, TN 37211

Sales and repair of new, new-old-stock,
    reproduction or rebuilt radios, speakers and
    boosters.

42
Auto Accessories of America
Box 427, Route 322
Boalsburg, PA 16827

New, used, new-old-stock, reproduction or rebuilt
   parts and services.
Camaros from 1967 to present.
Catalog, $5.00.

43
Auto Acres
Box 528
Lander, WY 82520

New, used, new-old-stock or reproduction parts and
   services.
All 1911–54 models of cars and trucks, excluding
   Corvettes.
Mechanical parts, accessories, body parts, interior
   parts, trim, chrome, electrical parts, hardware
   and other general parts.
All models.

44
Auto Body Specialties
Route 66, P.O. Box 455
Middlefield, CT 06455

New, used, new-old-stock, reproduction or rebuilt
   body and body trim parts.
Catalog, $4.00.

45
Auto Hardware Specialties
Route 1, Box 12A-C
Sheldon, IA 51201

New, new-old-stock or reproduction trim sources,
   bolts, fasteners and miscellaneous hardware.
Any model.
Catalog, $2.00.

46
Auto Krafters
Box 392
Timberville, VA 22853

Mechanical parts, accessories, body parts, interior
parts, trim, chrome, electrical parts, hardware
and other general parts; manuals, parts books,
price books, catalogs and other literature.
All models, all years.

47
Automotive Engine
845 South Montana
Butte, MT 59702

New, used, new-old-stock, reproduction or rebuilt
engines, powerplant parts and so on.

48
Automotive Information Clearing House
Box 1746
La Mesa, CA 92041

Manuals, parts books, price books, catalogs and
other literature.

49
Automotive Legal Service
P.O. Box 626
Dresher, PA 19025

Appraisals and estimates.
All models and eras.

50
Automotive Obsolete
1023 East 4th Street
Santa Ana, CA 92701

Mechanical parts, accessories, body parts, interior
parts, trim, chrome, electrical parts, hardware
and other general parts; manuals, parts books,
price books, catalogs and other literature.
All models, all years.

51

Automotive Paints Unlimited: The Paint Place
Route 1, Box 108T
Roxboro, NC 27573

Color-matching paint and dyes; acrylic enamels,
    lacquers, and so on.
All models from 1925 to present.

52

Automotive Restorations, Inc.
1785 Barnum Avenue
Stratford, CT 06497

Rebuilding, reconditioning, fabrication or
    restoration services.

53

Automotive Specialties
13723 Balm-Picnic Road
Wimauma, FL 33598

Rebuilding, reconditioning, fabrication or
    restoration services.

54

Automotive Wholesale
1018 Oldfield Point Road
Elkton, MD 21921

New, used, new-old-stock, reproduction or rebuilt
    engines, powerplant parts and so on, and
    suspension parts, supplies and services; brake
    parts.

55

Auto Parts Company
13450 West Michigan Avenue
Marshall, MN 49068

New, used, new-old-stock, reproduction or rebuilt
    high-performance parts and services.
Catalog, $3.00.

56
Auto Restoration Headquarters
I-49 and Highway 63
Rolla, MO 65401

Rebuilding, reconditioning, fabrication or
   restoration services.

57
Auto-Truck Springs
848 East Broadway
Muskegon, MI 49444

New, used, new-old-stock, reproduction or rebuilt
   suspension parts, supplies and services.

58
Bailey Brothers
4901 Nada-Vallejo Highway
Vallejo, CA 94589

New, used, new-old-stock, reproduction or rebuilt
   engines, powerplant parts and so on.

59
Bair's Corvettes
316 Franklin Street
Linesville, PA 16424

New, used, new-old-stock, reproduction or rebuilt
   parts and services.
Corvettes, all years.

60
Bakel Auto Machine
410 West 1st Street
Casa Grande, AZ 85222

New, used, new-old-stock, reproduction or rebuilt
   engines, powerplant parts and so on.

61
Banter's Chevrolet Parts
5904 Trouble Creek Road
New Port Richey, FL 34652

New, used, new-old-stock, reproduction or rebuilt
   parts and services.
Pickups and trucks, all years.

62
Bare Enterprises
P.O. Box 272271
Tampa, FL 33688

New, used, new-old-stock, reproduction or rebuilt
   parts and services.
Camaros from 1967 to present.
Free catalog.

63
Batista Chastain Restorations
5642 Mission Boulevard
Ontario, CA 91762

Rebuilding, reconditioning, fabrication or
   restoration services.

64
Benchmark Marketing
1243 South 119th Street
Omaha, NE 68144

Location, purchasing, selling and trading of cars
   and parts.
All models.

65
Bill Bonhams Chevy Parts & Accessories
Route 2, Box 260A
Vinton, VA 24179

New, used, new-old-stock, reproduction or rebuilt
   parts and services.
Chevelles, El Caminos and Malibus from 1964 to
   present.

66
Bill Cotrofeld Automotive Enterprises
East Arlington, VT 05252

New, used, new-old-stock, reproduction or rebuilt
    parts and services.
Corvairs, all years.

67
Bill Mock
Route 2, Box 140
Bartlesville, OK 74006

New, used, new-old-stock, reproduction or rebuilt
    cooling system parts and services.

68
Bill Reid
113 Bay Road
Brookhaven, NY 11719

Interior fabric, hardware and trim.

69
Bill's Speed Shop
13951 Millersburg SW
Navarre, OH 44662

New, used, new-old-stock, reproduction or rebuilt
    body and body trim parts.
Catalog, $4.00.

70
Bill Vos
2905 Moore Lane
Fort Collins, CO 80526

New, used, new-old-stock or reproduction parts and
    services.
All 1955–57 models, excluding Corvettes.
Send SASE and specify needs.

71
B. J. Wilkinson
3161 Dothan
Memphis, TN 38118

Mechanical parts, accessories, body parts, interior
parts, trim, chrome, electrical parts, hardware
and other general parts.
All models from 1958 to present.

72
Blue Ribbon Products, Limited
4965 Old House Trail NE
Atlanta, GA 30342

New, used, new-old-stock, reproduction or rebuilt
parts and services.
Corvettes, all years.
Free catalog.

73
Bob Cook Classic Custom Carpet
Department C/C
Hazel, KY 42049

Interior fabric, hardware and trim.

74
Bob Kunz
5959 Keller Road
St. Louis, MO 63128

New, new-old-stock, reproduction or rebuilt fuel
system parts and services.
Send SASE and specify needs.

75
Bob's
105 Sheldon
El Segundo, CA 90245

Parts, accessories, body parts, interior parts, trim,
chrome, electrical parts, hardware and other
general parts.
All models from 1955 to present.
Send SASE and specify needs.

76
Bob's Vette & Performance Center
901 Calumet Avenue
Valparaiso, IN 46383

New, used, new-old-stock, reproduction or rebuilt
   high-performance and non-high-performance
   parts and services.
Corvettes, all years.

77
Body Framing (Scott Restorations)
14661 Lanark Street
Panorama City, CA 91402

New, used, new-old-stock, reproduction or rebuilt
   body and body trim parts; rebuilding,
   reconditioning, fabrication or restoration services.

78
Borla East
600A Lincoln Boulevard
Middlesex, NJ 08846

New, new-old-stock or reproduction exhaust parts
   or complete systems.

79
Bowtie Barn
709 North Williams
Paulding, OH 45879

New, used, new-old-stock, reproduction or rebuilt
   parts and services.
Camaros from 1967 to present; Chevelles, El
   Caminos and Malibus from 1964 to present.

80
Bowtie Supply
1123 Lovejoy
Buffalo, NY 14206

New, used, new-old-stock, reproduction or rebuilt
   parts and services.
Chevelles, El Caminos and Malibus from 1964 to
   present.

81
Branson Enterprises
7722 Elm Avenue
Rockford, IL 61111

Sales and service of magnetos; new, used, new-old-
stock, reproduction or rebuilt high-performance
parts and services.

82
Brien's Corvette Enterprises
P.O. Box 5296
Arvado, CO 80005–0296
New, used, new-old-stock or reproduction cosmetic
and mechanical accessories.
All models and eras.
New, used, new-old-stock, reproduction or rebuilt
parts and services.
Corvettes, all years.

83
Bright Metal Polishing, Inc.
410 Florence Avenue
Hillside, NJ 07205

Chrome, cadmium and silver plating; metal
polishing; and so on.

84
Broadway Restoration
P.O. Box 535, Highway 57
Broadway, NJ 08808

Rebuilding, reconditioning, fabrication or
restoration services.

85
Bronson's Restoration
Box 112
Titonka, IA 50480

Rebuilding, reconditioning, fabrication or
restoration services.

86
Bronx Automotive
501 Tiffany Street
Bronx, NY 10474

Mechanical parts, accessories, body parts, interior
    parts, trim, chrome, electrical parts, hardware
    and other general parts.
All models, all years.

87
Bruce Falk
1105–H Nicholson
Joliet, IL 60435

New, used, new-old-stock or reproduction parts and
    services.
All 1911–54 models of cars and trucks, excluding
    Corvettes.

88
Bruce Horkey Cabinetry
Route 4, Box 188
Windom, MN 56101

New, used, new-old-stock, reproduction or rebuilt
    parts and services; custom wood beds.
Pickups and trucks, all years.
Catalog, $2.00.

89
Bryan Corvette Sales
1663 Armory Drive
Franklin, VA 23851

Location, purchasing, selling and trading of cars
    and parts.
All models.
New, used, new-old-stock, reproduction or rebuilt
    parts and services.
Corvettes, all years.

90
B. Small
230 Buena Vista
Fair Haven, NJ 07701

New, used, new-old-stock or reproduction cosmetic
and mechanical accessories; Continental kits;
new, used, new-old-stock, reproduction or rebuilt
body and body trim parts.
All models and eras.

91
B&T Truck Parts
P.O. Box 799
Siloam Springs, AR 72761

New, used, new-old-stock, reproduction or rebuilt
parts and services.
Pickups and trucks, all years.
Catalog, $3.00.

92
Burton Waldron
Box C
Nottawa, MI 49075

New, new-old-stock or reproduction exhaust parts
or complete systems.

93
Butch Rodgers
82 South Richard
Pine Bluff, AR 71602

New, used, new-old-stock, reproduction or rebuilt
parts and services.
Chevelles, El Caminos and Malibus from 1964 to
present.
Send SASE for catalog.

94
By the Yard
4105 East San Gabriel Avenue
Phoenix, AZ 85044

Interior fabric, hardware and trim.
Send fabric samples.

95
Cal West Radiators
201 South Anderson Street
Los Angeles, CA 90033

New, used, new-old-stock, reproduction or rebuilt
  cooling system parts and services.
Dealer inquiries welcome.

96
CALYX Manifold Dressing
P.O. Box 39277
Cincinnati, OH 45239

Exhaust manifold coating.

97
CAM
808 West Vermont Avenue
Anaheim, CA 92635

Sales and repair of new, new-old-stock, reproduction or rebuilt radios, speakers and boosters.

98
Camaro Connections
34B Cleveland
Bay Shore, NY 11706

New, used, new-old-stock, reproduction or rebuilt
  parts and services.
Camaros from 1967 to present.

99
Camaro Country
18591 Centennial Road
Marshall, MI 49068

New, used, new-old-stock, reproduction or rebuilt
  parts and services.
Camaros from 1967 to present.
Catalog, $3.00.

100
Camaro Headquarters
1012 Easton Road
Roslyn, PA 19001

New, used, new-old-stock, reproduction or rebuilt
    parts and services.
Camaros from 1967 to present.
Dealer inquiries welcome.

101
Camaro Owners of America, Inc.
Department 20
701 North Keyser Avenue
Scranton, PA 18508

Restoration, preservation and collection.
Any model.

102
Camaro Specialties
Bob and June Harris
898 East Filmore, CC
East Aurora, NY 14052

New, used, new-old-stock, reproduction or rebuilt
    parts and services.
Camaros from 1967 to present.

103
Camwerks Corporation
5128 East 65th Street
Indianapolis, IN 46220

Camshafts ground to original specifications.

104
Cannon's Recycled Parts
860 West 44th Street
Norfolk, VA 23508

New, used, new-old-stock, reproduction or rebuilt
    parts and services.
Corvettes, all years.

105
Capitol Corvette
5400 King James Way
Madison, WI 53719

New, used, new-old-stock, reproduction or rebuilt
    parts and services.
Corvettes, all years.

106
Carbs Unlimited
19332 Briarwood
Mount Clemens, MI 48043

New, new-old-stock, reproduction or rebuilt fuel
    system parts and services.

107
Carburetor Engineering
3324 East Colorado
Pasadena, CA 91107

New, new-old-stock, reproduction or rebuilt fuel
    system parts and services.

108
Carburetor Shop
1457 Philadelphia, Suite 24
Ontario, CA 91761

New, new-old-stock, reproduction or rebuilt fuel
    system parts and services.
Catalog, $2.00.

109
Car Connection
164 Route 3A
Lake Cohasset, MA 02025

Location, purchasing, selling and trading of cars
    and parts.
All models.

110
Carfind
P.O. Box 7146
Endicott, NY 13760

Location, purchasing, selling and trading of cars
and parts.
All models.

111
Carl's Classic Chevy Parts
P.O. Box 1150
Allentown, PA 18105-1150

Mechanical parts, accessories, body parts, interior
parts, trim, chrome, electrical parts, hardware
and other general parts.
All models, all years.

112
Carolina Cadillacs
Route 2, Box 212
Ayden, NC 28513

Mechanical parts, accessories, body parts, interior
parts, trim, chrome, electrical parts, hardware
and other general parts.
All models from 1960 to present.
Send SASE for catalog.

113
Carolina Camaro
Route 3, Box 24
Elon College, NC 27244

New, used, new-old-stock, reproduction or rebuilt
parts and services.
Camaros from 1967 to present.
Catalog, $2.00.

114
Cars, Inc.
1964 West 11 Mile Road
Department HM9
Berkley, MI 48072

New, used, new-old-stock, reproduction or rebuilt parts and services.

Camaros from 1967 to present; Chevelles, El Caminos and Malibus from 1964 to present; full-sized models (i.e., BelAirs, Biscaynes, Caprices, Impalas, station wagons and so on); Monte Carlos from 1970 to present; Novas and Chevy IIs from 1962 to present.

Interior fabric, hardware and trim.

Catalog, $3.00.

115
Carson's
235 Shawfarm
Holliston, MA 01746

New, used, new-old-stock, reproduction or rebuilt engines, powerplant parts and so on.

116
Cars and Stripes
2712 Canary Place
Mesquite, TX 75149

New, used, new-old-stock, reproduction or rebuilt parts and services.

Chevelles, El Caminos and Malibus from 1964 to present; Monte Carlos from 1970 to present.

117
CAT
45 Swan Street
Pawtucket, RI 02860

New, used, new-old-stock, reproduction or rebuilt parts and services.

Camaros from 1967 to present.

118
C&C Automotive Reproductions
2742 Stafford Court
New Carlisle, OH 45344

Mechanical parts, accessories, body parts, interior
parts, trim, chrome, electrical parts, hardware
and other general parts.
All models, all years.
Dealer inquiries welcome.

119
C&C Classics
Box 628
Carver, MA 02330

New, used, new-old-stock, reproduction or rebuilt
parts and services.
Novas and Chevy IIs from 1962 to present.
Send SASE for catalog.

120
Central Pennsylvania Corvair Club
1751 Chesley Road
York, PA 17403

Restoration, preservation and collection.
Any model.

121
Central Radiator Works
1981 South Lake Drive
Lexington, SC 29072

New, used, new-old-stock, reproduction or rebuilt
cooling system parts and services.
Catalog, $2.00.

122
Charles Seigfried
2530 Pleasanthill Road
Sebastopol, CA 95472

Sales and repair of new, new-old-stock,
reproduction or rebuilt radios, speakers and
boosters.

123
Charles Walcutt
6 Valleywood Court
Timonium, MD 21093

Title location and securement.

124
Chasers Antique Car Parts
P.O. Box 552
Lawrence, KS 66044

Mechanical parts, accessories, body parts, interior
   parts, trim, chrome, electrical parts, hardware
   and other general parts.
All models, all years.

125
Chevelle Center
45C Mason Street
Salem, MA 01970

New, used, new-old-stock, reproduction or rebuilt
   parts and services.
Chevelles, El Caminos and Malibus from 1964 to
   present.

126
Chevelle Classics
16602 Burke Lane
Huntington Beach, CA 92647

New, used, new-old-stock, reproduction or rebuilt
   parts and services.
Chevelles, El Caminos and Malibus from 1964 to
   present.
Catalog, $2.00.

127
Chevelle King Auto Parts
18653 Ventura Boulevard, Suite 708
Tarzana, CA 91536

New, used, new-old-stock, reproduction or rebuilt
   parts and services.

Chevelles, El Caminos and Malibus from 1964 to
   present.
Free catalog.

128
Chevelle World
Box 38
Department HR1
Washington, OK 73093

New, used, new-old-stock, reproduction or rebuilt
   parts and services.
Chevelles, El Caminos and Malibus from 1964 to
   present.
Catalog, $2.00.

129
Chevrolet Carpet and Trim
1981 South Lake Drive
Lexington, SC 29072

Interior fabric, hardware and trim.

130
Chevrolet Specialties
4335 South Highland Avenue
Butler, PA 16001

New, used, new-old-stock, reproduction or rebuilt
   parts and services.
Chevelles, El Caminos and Malibus from 1964 to
   present.

131
Chevs of the 40's
18409 Northeast 28th Street #1
Vancouver, WA 98662

New, used, new-old-stock or reproduction parts
   and services.
All 1911–54 models of cars and trucks, excluding
   Corvettes.
Catalog, $3.25.

34

132
Chevycraft
3414 Quirt
Lubbock, TX 79407

Mechanical parts, accessories, body parts, interior
   parts, trim, chrome, electrical parts, hardware
   and other general parts.
All models from 1955 to present.

133
Chevy Duty Truck Parts
4600 Northwest 52nd Street
Kansas City, MO 64151

New, used, new-old-stock, reproduction or rebuilt
   parts and services.
Pickups and trucks, all years.
Catalog, $1.00; specify year.

134
Chevyland
3667 Recycle Road, Suite 8
Department BG
Rancho Cordova, CA 95670

New, used, new-old-stock, reproduction or rebuilt
   parts and services.
Chevelles, El Caminos and Malibus from 1964 to
   present; Corvettes, all years.

135
Chevy Parts
Box 936
Greensburg, KS 67054

New, used, new-old-stock or reproduction parts
   and services.
All 1911–54 models of cars and trucks, excluding
   Corvettes.

136
Chevy Rolls Out the Thunder (Crott Club)
4613 Craftsbury Circle
Fort Wayne, IN 46818
Restoration, preservation and collection.
Any model.

137
Chevy World
P.O. Box 115
Sawyer, MI 49125

Mechanical parts, accessories, body parts, interior
    parts, trim, chrome, electrical parts, hardware
    and other general parts.
All models, all years.
Free catalog.

138
Chewnings Auto Literature, Limited
Box 727
Broadway, VA 22815

Manuals, parts books, price books, catalogs and
    other literature.

139
Chicago Auto
2425 South Wood
Chicago, IL 60608

Mechanical parts, accessories, body parts, interior
    parts, trim, chrome, electrical parts, hardware
    and other general parts.
All models from 1960 to present.

140
Chicago Camaro and Firebird
900 South 5th
Maywood, IL 60153

New, used, new-old-stock, reproduction or rebuilt
    parts and services.
Camaros from 1967 to present.

141
Chicago Corvette Supply
8260 Archer Avenue
Willow Springs, IL 60480

New, used, new-old-stock, reproduction or rebuilt
parts and services.
Corvettes, all years.
New, new-old-stock, reproduction or rebuilt fuel
system parts and services.

142
Chicago Metallizing Corporation
2628 South Sacramento
Chicago, IL 60623

Chrome, cadmium and silver plating; metal
polishing; and so on.

143
Chirco Automotive
9101 East 22nd Street
Tucson, AZ 85710

New, new-old-stock, reproduction or rebuilt fuel
system parts and services.

144
Chrome Company Inc.
744 North Indiana Street
Elmhurst, IL 60126

New, used, new-old-stock or reproduction cosmetic
and mechanical accessories; new, used, new-old-
stock, reproduction or rebuilt engines,
powerplant parts and so on.
All models and eras.

145
Chuck Scharf Enterprises
813 South Valley
New Ulm, MN 56073

New, used, new-old-stock, reproduction or rebuilt
parts and services; 348/409 engines, powerplant

parts and so on.

1958–65 full-sized models (i.e., BelAirs, Biscaynes, Caprices, Impalas, station wagons and so on).

146
Chuck Smith
2260 Cold Canyon Road
Calabasas, CA 91302

New, new-old-stock, reproduction or rebuilt fuel system parts and services.

147
Ciadella Enterprises, Inc.
3757 East Broadway Road #4HSC
Phoenix, AZ 85044

Interior fabric, hardware and trim.
Catalog, $3.00.

148
Cincinnati Woodworks
1974 Central Avenue
Cincinnati, OH 45219

New, used, new-old-stock, reproduction or rebuilt body and body trim parts.

149
City of Firsts Classic Chevy Club
2905 Mill Street
Kokomo, IN 46902

Restoration, preservation and collection.
Any model.

150
CJ Auto
Route 5, Box 116
Littleton, NC 27850

New, used, new-old-stock, reproduction or rebuilt parts and services.

Chevelles, El Caminos and Malibus from 1964 to present.

151
Clark's Corvair Parts, Inc.
Route 2
Shelburne, MA 01370

New, used, new-old-stock, reproduction or rebuilt
    parts and services.
Corvairs, all years.
Catalog, $4.00.

152
Clarkson
1233 Saint Andrew's
Waterloo, IA 50701

Mechanical parts, accessories, body parts, interior
    parts, trim, chrome, electrical parts, hardware
    and other general parts.
All models, 1933–69.
Send SASE; specify year and model.

153
Classic Auto Air Manufacturing Company
2020 West Kennedy Boulevard
Tampa, FL 33506

New, new-old-stock, reproduction and rebuilt
    classic auto air conditioning, parts and service.

154
Classic Auto Restoration
404 Home Street
Mercer, PA 16137

Mechanical parts, accessories, body parts, interior
    parts, trim, chrome, electrical parts, hardware
    and other general parts; rebuilding,
    reconditioning, fabrication or restoration services.
All models, all years.

155
Classic Camaro Parts and Accessories, Inc.
16651 Gemini Lane
Huntington Beach, CA 92647

New, used, new-old-stock, reproduction or rebuilt
    parts and services.
Camaros from 1967 to present.
Catalog, $2.00.

156
Classic Car Centre
Route 7, Box 43
Warsaw, IN 46580

Rebuilding, reconditioning, fabrication or
    restoration services.

157
Classic Car Fair, Inc.
1620 West 98th Street, Suite D
Bloomington, MN 55431

New, new-old-stock or reproduction weather
    stripping, moldings, gaskets, seals and other
    rubber parts.
Dealer inquiries welcome.

158
Classic Car Investments
4601 New Bern Avenue
Raleigh, NC 27610

Location, purchasing, selling and trading of cars
    and parts; mechanical parts, accessories, body
    parts, interior parts, trim, chrome, electrical
    parts, hardware and other general parts.
All models, all years.

159
Classic Car Parts
4837 Auburn Boulevard
Sacramento, CA 95841

Mechanical parts, accessories, body parts, interior
    parts, trim, chrome, electrical parts, hardware
    and other general parts.
All models from 1955 to present.
Catalog, $3.75.

160
Classic Cars
10 Tipping Drive
Branford, CT 06405

New, used, new-old-stock, reproduction or rebuilt
cooling system parts and services.

161
Classic Chevy Club International
P.O. Box 17188
Orlando, FL 32860

Restoration, preservation and collection.
Any model.

162
Classic Engine Company
Oshkosh, WI 54901

Head and block rebuilding, reconditioning or
fabrication.

163
Classic Glass, Inc.
287 Salem Street
Woburn, MA 01801

New, new-old-stock or reproduction windows,
windshields and other glass parts.
All models and years.

164
Classic GM Specialists
3214 East Milber
Tucson, AZ 85714

Mechanical parts, accessories, body parts, interior
parts, trim, chrome, electrical parts, hardware
and other general parts.
All models, all years.

165
Classic Motorbooks
P.O. Box 1/HM019
Osceola, WI 54020

Manuals, parts books, price books, catalogs and
other literature.
Free catalog with order.

166
Classic Motor Cars
2524 South Minnesota
Sioux Falls, SD 57100

Location, purchasing, selling and trading of cars
and parts.
All models.

167
Classic Motoring Accessories
146 West Pomona Avenue, Suite S
Monrovia, CA 91016

New, used, new-old-stock or reproduction cosmetic
and mechanical accessories.
All models and eras.

168
Classic Reproductions
807 23rd Street
Rockford, IL 61108

New, used, new-old-stock, reproduction or rebuilt
parts and services.
Chevelles, El Caminos and Malibus from 1964 to
present.
Interior fabric, hardware and trim; new, new-old-
stock or reproduction weather stripping,
moldings, gaskets, seals and other rubber parts.

169
Classic Restorations Unlimited
Lee Forest
134 Maple Street
Manchester, NH 03103

Rebuilding, reconditioning, fabrication or
restoration services.
Send SASE for catalog.

170
Classic Rubber Products
East 539 North Park Street
Lake City, MI 49651

New, new-old-stock or reproduction weather
stripping, moldings, gaskets, seals and other
rubber parts.

171
Classic Stainless Components Corporation
16715 West Park Circle Drive
Chagrin Falls, OH 44022

New, new-old-stock or reproduction trim sources,
bolts, fasteners and miscellaneous hardware.
Any model.

172
Classy Chassis Autoworks
1218 East 14th Street
Lombard, IL 60148

Manuals, parts books, price books, catalogs and
other literature.
Send SASE for catalog.

173
Cliffs Classic Chevy Parts Company
P.O. Box 16739
619 Southeast 202nd
Portland, OR 97216-0739

New, used, new-old-stock or reproduction parts and
services.
All 1955-57 models, excluding Corvettes.
Catalog, $3.50.

174
The Clock Shop
4141 Monroe Street
Toledo, OH 43606

Clock repair.

175
Coast Camaro
P.O. Box 16127
Department HR–1
Irvine, CA 92713

New, used, new-old-stock, reproduction or rebuilt
    parts and services.
Camaros from 1967 to present.
Catalog, $2.00.

176
Coffman Corvette
1472 U.S. 42, Route 11
Mansfield, OH 44903

New, used, new-old-stock, reproduction or rebuilt
    parts and services.
Corvettes, all years.

177
Coil Spring Specialties
2322 Bates Avenue, Unit V-CR
Concord, CA 94520

New, used, new-old-stock, reproduction or rebuilt
    suspension parts, supplies and services.

178
Coker Tire
1317 Chestnut Street
P.O. Box 72554
Chattanooga, TN 37407

New, new-old-stock or reproduction antique and
    classic tires.

179
Comparts, USA
1802 West 2250 South
Syracuse, UT 84075

Location, purchasing, selling and trading of cars
    and parts.
All models.

44

180
Computerized Auto Parts Search
P.O. Box 2755
Warminster, PA 18974

Location, purchasing, selling and trading of cars
and parts.
All models.

181
Condon & Skelly
121 East Kines Highway, Suite 203
Maple Shade, NJ 08052

Insurance for antique and restored vehicles.

182
Continental Enterprises
1673 Cary Road
Kelowna, British Columbia, Canada VIX 2C1

Continental kits.
Catalog, $2.00.

183
Convertible King
Box 2593
Framingham, MA 01701

New, used, new-old-stock, reproduction or rebuilt
parts and services.
Convertibles, all years.

184
Convertible Service
5126 H Walnut Grove Avenue
San Gabriel, CA 91776

New, used, new-old-stock, reproduction or rebuilt
parts and services.
Convertibles, all years.

185
Corvair Society of America
2506 Gross Point Road
Evanston, IL 60201

Listing of clubs involved with restoration,
preservation or collection.
Any model.

186
Corvair Underground
P.O. Box 404
Hillsboro, OR 97123

New, used, new-old-stock, reproduction or rebuilt
parts and services.
Corvairs, all years.
Catalog, $4.00.

187
Corvair Warehouse
1506 Blackstone
Fresno, CA 93703

New, used, new-old-stock, reproduction or rebuilt
parts and services.
Corvairs, all years.
Send SASE for catalog.

188
Corvette Accessories and Service
2313 East Washington Street
Indianapolis, IN 46201

New, used, new-old-stock, reproduction or rebuilt
parts and services.
All years.

189
Corvette America
Box 427, Route 322
Boalsburg, PA 16827

New, used, new-old-stock, reproduction or rebuilt
parts and services.
Corvettes, all years.
Catalog, $5.00.

190
Corvette Avenue
P.O. Box 5158
Parsippany, NJ 07054

New, used, new-old-stock, reproduction or rebuilt
   parts and services.
Corvettes, all years.
Free catalog.

191
Corvette Center
5930 Padnia Court
Colorado Springs, CO 80915

New, used, new-old-stock, reproduction or rebuilt
   parts and services.
Corvettes, all years.
Free catalog.

192
Corvette Central
P.O. Box 16, Sawyer Street
Sawyer, MI 49125

New, used, new-old-stock, reproduction or rebuilt
   parts and services.
Corvettes, all years.
Catalog, $3.00.

193
Corvette Clinics
2870 Skokie Valley Highway
Highland Park, IL 60035

New, used, new-old-stock, reproduction or rebuilt
   parts and services.
Corvettes, all years.
Rebuilding, reconditioning, fabrication or
   restoration services.

194
Corvette Clocks by Roger
3216 West Boulevard
Belleville, IL 62221

Clock repair.
Corvettes.
Catalog, $1.00.

195
The Corvette Cluster
4622 West Browning Avenue
Tampa, FL 33629

Sales and repair of new, used, new-old-stock,
    reproduction or rebuilt clocks and gauges.
Corvettes.

196
Corvette Connection, Inc.
12581 Metro Parkway #4
Fort Myers, FL 33912

New, used, new-old-stock, reproduction or rebuilt
    parts and services.
Corvettes, all years.

197
Corvette Consultants (RPE Limited)
328 Virginia Road
Concord, MA 01742

Appraisals and estimates.
All models and eras.
New, used, new-old-stock, reproduction or rebuilt
    parts and services.
Corvettes, all years.

198
Corvette Corner Inc.
3245 Morse Road
Columbus, OH 43216

New, used, new-old-stock, reproduction or rebuilt
    parts and services.
Corvettes, all years.

199

Corvette Cosmetics
1228 South Jackson Street, Suite C
Fort Smith, AR 72901

New, used, new-old-stock, reproduction or rebuilt
parts and services.
Corvettes, all years.

200

Corvette Performance Products
P.O. Box 6421
Evansville, IN 47719

New, used, new-old-stock, reproduction or rebuilt
parts and services.
Corvettes, all years.

201

Corvette Rubber Company
H-533 North Park Street
Lake City, MI 49651

New, used, new-old-stock, reproduction or rebuilt
parts and services.
Corvettes, all years.
New, new-old-stock or reproduction weather
stripping, moldings, gaskets, seals and other
rubber parts.
Free catalog.

202

Corvettes Northwest
121 Duryea
Raymond, WA 98577

New, used, new-old-stock, reproduction or rebuilt
parts and services.
Corvettes, all years.
Interior fabric, hardware and trim.
Free catalog.

203

Corvette Specialized Parts & Services
4492 Quarterhorse Drive
Roswell, GA 30075

New, used, new-old-stock, reproduction or rebuilt
parts and services.
Corvettes, all years.

204

Corvette Specialties Manufacturing
3422 Pine Circle S
Westminster, MD 21157

New, used, new-old-stock, reproduction or rebuilt
parts and services.
Corvettes, all years.

205

Corvette Specialties of Maryland
3422 Pine Circle
Westminster, MD 21157

New, used, new-old-stock, reproduction or rebuilt
parts and services; sales and repair of new, used,
new-old-stock, reproduction or rebuilt clocks and
gauges.
Corvettes, all years.

206

Corvette Specialty Center, Inc.
Route 52
Walden, NY 12586

New, used, new-old stock, reproduction or rebuilt
parts and services.
Corvettes, all years.
Rebuilding, reconditioning, fabrication or
restoration services.
Catalog, $3.00.

207

Corvette Sports, Inc.
720 Forest Avenue
Sheboygan Falls, WI 53085

New, used, new-old-stock, reproduction or rebuilt
parts and services.
Corvettes, all years.

208

Corvette Stainless Steel Brakes, Inc.
4041 Northwest 25th Street
Miami, FL 33142

New, used, new-old-stock, reproduction or rebuilt
brake parts.
Corvettes.

209

Corvette Stop, Inc.
230 North Harrison Avenue
Campbell, CA 95008

New, used, new-old-stock, reproduction or rebuilt
parts and services.
Corvettes, all years.
Rebuilding, reconditioning, fabrication or
restoration services.

210

Corvette Supplies by Midamerica
P.O. Box 1368
Department NB068
Effingham, IL 62401

New, used, new-old-stock, reproduction or rebuilt
parts and services.
Corvettes, all years.
Catalog, $3.00.

211

Corvette Warehouse
204 Industry Parkway
Old Bluegrass Strip
Nicholasville, KY 40356

New, used, new-old-stock, reproduction or rebuilt
parts and services.
Corvettes, all years.

212
Cosworth Vega Owners Association
5603 Edwards
Arungton, TX 76017

Restoration, preservation and collection.
Any model.

213
C&P
Box 348C
Kulpsville, PA 19443

New, used, new-old-stock or reproduction parts and
    services.
All 1955–57 models, excluding Corvettes.
Free catalog.

214
Cranes Corvette Supply
San Diego, CA

New, used, new-old-stock, reproduction or rebuilt
    parts and services.
Corvettes, all years.
Free catalog.

215
Custom Aluminum Coating
9030 Emnora Lane
Houston, TX 77080

Chrome, cadmium and silver plating; metal
    polishing; and so on.

216
Custom Audio Products
20265 Valley Boulevard
Walnut, CA 91789

Sales and repair of new, new-old-stock,
    reproduction or rebuilt radios, speakers and
    boosters.

217
Custom Auto Sound Manufacturing, Inc.
808 West Vermont Avenue
Anaheim, CA 92805

Sales and repair of new, new-old-stock,
reproduction or rebuilt radios, speakers and
boosters.

218
Custom Mold Dynamics, Inc.
5161 Wolfpen Pleasant Hill Road
Department SC
Milford, OH 45150

New, used, new-old-stock, reproduction or rebuilt
body and body trim parts; interior hardware and
trim.
Catalog, $3.00.

219
Custom Plating
1253 Sheppard Court
Stone Mountain, GA 30083

Chrome, cadmium and silver plating; metal
polishing; and so on.

220
Cylinder Head Abrasives
2120 Blumenfeld Drive
Sacramento, CA 95815

Special tools and machinery for restoration and
preservation.
Free catalog.

221
DA Brake Supply
Kettela Avenue
Anaheim, CA 92803

New, used, new-old-stock, reproduction or rebuilt
brake and suspension parts, supplies and
services.

222
D&A Corvette, Inc.
Route 2, Box 15
Gillespie, IL 62033

Location, purchasing, selling and trading of cars
and parts.
All models.
New, used, new-old-stock, reproduction or rebuilt
parts and services.
Corvettes, all years.
Catalog, $5.00.

223
Dagley's
2454 South 35th Avenue
Phoenix, AZ 85075

Mechanical parts, accessories, body parts, interior
parts, trim, chrome, electrical parts, hardware
and other general parts.
All 1964–81 models.

224
Dakota Motor Car Sales
41st and Minnesota Avenue
Sioux Falls, SD 57100

Location, purchasing, selling and trading of cars
and parts.
All models.

225
Dale Shafer
1310 North Cedar
Hastings, NE 68901

New, used, new-old-stock, reproduction or rebuilt
parts and services.
Chevelles, El Caminos and Malibus from 1964 to
present.

226
Dale Wilch Sales Co, Inc.
Department DOW
4925 State Avenue
Kansas City, KS 66102

New, used, new-old-stock, reproduction or rebuilt
   high-performance parts and services.
Catalog, $2.00.

227
Danchuk Manufacturing
3221 South Halladay Street
Department HMNP
Santa Ana, CA 92705

New, used, new-old-stock, reproduction or rebuilt
   parts and services.
All 1955–57 models, excluding Corvettes; Chevelles,
   El Caminos and Malibus from 1964 to present.
Catalog, $7.00.

228
Dan Packard
8 Florence Road
Marblehead, MA 01945

Sales and repair of new, new-old-stock,
   reproduction or rebuilt radios, speakers and
   boosters.

229
Dan's Classics
40 Southeast 28th
Portland, OR 97214

New, used, new-old-stock, reproduction or rebuilt
   parts and services.
Chevelles, El Caminos and Malibus from 1964 to
   present; pickups and trucks, all years.
Truck catalog, $1.50.

230
Darren DeSantis
67 Lou Ann Drive
Depew, NY 14043

Sun visor upholstering.

231
Daryll's Gear Box
633 Southfield Road
Lincoln Park, MI 48146

New, used, new-old-stock, reproduction or rebuilt
transmissions or parts.

232
Dave Sylvain
18 South Gate Circle
North Franklin, CT 06254

New, used, new-old-stock or reproduction parts and
services.
All models of cars and trucks, excluding Corvettes.
Computer list available.

233
David Bailey
15609 East 44th Street
Independence, MO 64055

New, used, new-old-stock, reproduction or rebuilt
parts and services.
Pickups and trucks, all years.
Free catalog.

234
David R. Cosner
316 Forestview Drive
Bedford, IN 47421

Wheels and wheel accessories.
Corvettes.

235
David Evanclew, Inc.
5661 Rome-Taberg Road
Rome, NY 13440

Frame and floorboard fabrication.

236
David Lindquist
12427 Penn
Whittier, CA 90602

Clock repair.
All models.

237
David Stewman Company
Route 4, Chevy Drive
Mena, AR 71953

New, used, new-old-stock, reproduction or rebuilt
    parts and services.
1947–54 pickups and trucks.
Free catalog.

238
DCE Auto Air
6062 East Lancaster
Fort Worth, TX 76112

New, used, new-old-stock, reproduction or rebuilt
    cooling and air-conditioning system parts and
    services.

239
D&D Auto Transport, Inc.
103 Hunter Lane, Route 2
Smyrna, TN 37167

Automobile transportation.

240
D&D Clutch and Brake
3151 Cooper Street
Punta Gorda, FL 33950

New, used, new-old-stock, reproduction or rebuilt
brake parts, transmissions or transmission parts.

241
Delta Camshaft
1938 Tacoma Avenue South
Tacoma, WA 98402

Camshafts ground to original specifications.

242
Dennis Carpenter
P.O. Box 26398
Charlotte, NC 28221

New, used, new-old-stock, reproduction or rebuilt
parts and services.
Pickups and trucks, all years.

243
Dennis Portka
4326 Beetow Drive
Hamburg, NY 14075

Horn rebuilding.

244
Design-I Chevrolet
214 Riverside Boulevard
Loves Park, IL 61111

Mechanical parts, accessories, body parts, interior
parts, trim, chrome, electrical parts, hardware
and other general parts.
All models, all years.
Catalog, $2.00.

245
Details by Jay Nixon
601 West 8th Street
Muncie, IN 47302

New, used, new-old-stock, reproduction or rebuilt
parts and services.
Camaros from 1967 to present; Novas and Chevy IIs
from 1962 to present.
Restoration detail items.

246
De Witt's Corvettes
P.O. Box 32
Novi, MI 48050

New, used, new-old-stock, reproduction or rebuilt
parts and services.
Corvettes, all years.

247
Dick Evans
45 Prospect Street
Essex Junction, VT 05452
(May through October)

521 Wood Street
Dunedin, FL 34698
(October through May)

Temperature gauge repair.

248
Dillon's
2046 Brockett Road
Tucker, GA 30084

New, used, new-old-stock, reproduction or rebuilt
cooling system parts and services; interior fabric,
hardware and trim.

249
The Discount Book Company
P.O. Box 3150 BE
San Rafael, CA 94912-3150

Manuals, parts books, price books, catalogs and
other literature.
Catalog, $2.00.

250
Discount Parts and Pieces
P.O. Box 1120
Hillsborough, NC 27278

Mechanical parts, accessories, body parts, interior
  parts, trim, chrome, electrical parts, hardware
  and other general parts.
All models, all years.
Free catalog.

251
Dixie Truck Works
9233 Sandburg Avenue
Charlotte, NC 28213

New, used, new-old-stock, reproduction or rebuilt
  parts and services.
Pickups and trucks, all years.
Catalog, $3.00.

252
DK Corvettes
1062 West Birchwood
Mesa, AZ 85202

Rebuilding, reconditioning, fabrication or
  restoration services.
Corvettes.

253
D&L Corvette Supplies
191 B. Sheffield Drive
Danville, IN 46122

New, used, new-old-stock, reproduction or rebuilt
  parts and services.
Corvettes, all years.

254
D&M Corvette Specialist Limited
1804 Ogden Avenue
Downers Grove, IL 60515

New, used, new-old-stock, reproduction or rebuilt
parts and services; rebuilding, reconditioning,
fabrication or restoration services.
Corvettes, all years.
New, used, new-old-stock, reproduction or rebuilt
body and body trim parts; location, purchasing,
selling and trading of cars and parts.
All models.

255
D&M Restoration
504 Boston Post Road
East Lyme, CT 06333

Sales and repair of new, used, new old stock,
reproduction or rebuilt clocks and gauges.

256
Don Girton
Box 206
Stilesville, IN 46180

New, used, new-old-stock, reproduction or rebuilt
parts and services.
Chevelles, El Caminos and Malibus from 1964 to
present.

257
Don's Custom Exhaust
P.O. Box 157
Dover, OH 44622

New, new-old-stock or reproduction exhaust parts
or complete systems.
1969–72 Chevelle big-block tailpipes with
resonators.

258
Don Sears
1111 South 79th Street
Omaha, NE 68124

Sales and repair of new, used, new-old-stock,
reproduction or rebuilt clocks and gauges;
instrument refacing.

259
Don's East Coast Restoration
386 South 13th Street
Lindenhurst, NY 11757

New, used, new-old-stock, reproduction or rebuilt
    parts and services.
All 1955–57 models, excluding Corvettes; Chevelles,
    El Caminos and Malibus from 1964 to present.

260
Don's Obsolete Auto Parts
13059 Rosecrans
Santa Fe Springs, CA 90670

Mechanical parts, accessories, body parts, interior
    parts, trim, chrome, electrical parts, hardware
    and other general parts.
All models, all years.

261
Don Sumners—The Truck Shop
P.O. Box 5035
Department 1
102 West Marion Avenue
Nashville, GA 31639

New, used, new-old-stock, reproduction or rebuilt
    parts and services.
Pickups and trucks, all years.
Catalog, $3.00.

262
Don Watson
P.O. Box 1622
Upland, CA 91785

New, used, new-old-stock or reproduction parts and
    services.
All 1955–57 models, excluding Corvettes.

263
Douglas Vogel
1100 Shady Oaks
Ann Arbor, MI 48103

Manuals, parts books, price books, catalogs and other literature.

264
Doug Pollock
SMS
7700 Southeast 30th
Portland, OR 97202

Interior fabric, hardware and trim.

265
Doug's Auto Parts
Highway 59N, Box 811
Marshall, MN 56258

New, used, new-old-stock, reproduction or rebuilt body and body trim parts.
Catalog, $4.00.

266
Drake Restoration
4504 C Del Amo Boulevard
Torrance, CA 90500

New, used, new-old-stock or reproduction parts and services.
All 1955–57 models, excluding Corvettes.
Catalog, $1.00.

267
D&R Classic
2101 North 75th Avenue
Elmwood Park, IL 60635

New, used, new-old-stock, reproduction or rebuilt parts and services.
Camaros from 1967 to present; Chevelles, El Caminos and Malibus from 1964 to present.
Catalog, $1.00.

268
Dressen Custom Trailers, Inc.
Highway 77 South
Dell Rapids, SD 57022

Transport trailers and parts.

269
Driveline Service
600 North Weber
Sioux Falls, SD 57102

Driveline parts and services.

270
Dr. Rebuild
P.O. Box 6263
Bridgeport, CT 06606

Mechanical parts, accessories, body parts, interior
    parts, trim, chrome, electrical parts, hardware
    and other general parts; rebuilding,
    reconditioning, fabrication or restoration services.
All models, all years.
Catalog, $3.00.

271
Dr. Vette
212 7th Street SW
New Philadelphia, OH 34663

New, used, new-old-stock, reproduction or rebuilt
    brake parts.
Corvettes.

272
Dub's Supply
940 Middle Cove
Plano, TX 75023

New, used, new-old-stock, reproduction or rebuilt
    parts and services.
Chevelles, El Caminos and Malibus from 1964 to
    present; Corvettes, all years.

273
Duffy's Collectible Cars
250 Classic Car Court SW
Cedar Rapids, IA 52404

Location, purchasing, selling and trading of cars
    and parts.
All models.
Free brochure.

274
Eckler's Corvette Parts
P.O. Box 5637
Titusville, FL 32783

New, used, new-old-stock, reproduction or rebuilt
    parts and services.
Corvettes, all years.
Free catalog.

275
EC Products Design, Inc.
P.O. Box 2360
Atascadero, CA 93423

New, used, new-old-stock, reproduction or rebuilt
    parts and services.
Corvettes, all years.
Catalog, $3.00.

276
Edwards Brothers
14223 Hawthorne Court
Fountain Hills, AZ 85268

New, used, new-old-stock, reproduction or rebuilt
    brake parts, engines, powerplant parts and so on,
    and suspension parts, supplies and services.
Send SASE for free catalog.

277
Ed White Head & Block Repair
P.O. Box 968, Highway 33 East
Chouteau, OK 74337

Engine block and head repair.

278
Egge Machine Co
8403 Allport
Sante Fe Springs, CA 90670

New, used, new-old-stock, reproduction or rebuilt
   engines, powerplant parts and so on, and
   suspension parts, supplies and services.
Catalog, $1.50.

279
The El Camino Store
618 East Gutierrez Street
Department HMN
Santa Barbara, CA 93103

New, used, new-old-stock, reproduction or rebuilt
   parts and services.
Chevelles, El Caminos and Malibus from 1964 to
   present.
Catalog, $3.00.

280
Electro Plating Service
127 Oakley Avenue
White Plains, NY 10601

Chrome, cadmium and silver plating; metal
   polishing; and so on.

281
Elgin Auto Sales, Inc.
910 East Chicago Street
Elgin, IL 60120

New, used, new-old-stock, reproduction or rebuilt
   parts and services.
Corvettes, all years.
Location, purchasing, selling and trading of cars
   and parts.
All models.

282

Elmo's Grainmobile
Route 4, Box 262
Rusk, TX 75785

Custom wood graining.

283

Engine Dynamics
1535 Oke
Crete, NE 68333

New, used, new-old-stock, reproduction or rebuilt
engines, powerplant parts and so on.

284

Engineered Components, Inc.
P.O. Box 2361
Vernon, CT 06066

Disc brake conversions.

285

Engineering Plus
Box 337
League City, TX 77573

New, used, new-old-stock, reproduction or rebuilt
electrical system parts and services (i.e., batteries,
wiring kits and so on).

286

Engine Limited
821 Division Street
Oshkosh, WI 54901

New, used, new-old-stock, reproduction or rebuilt
engines, powerplant parts and so on.

287

Engine Parts Corporation
716 Stockton Avenue
San Jose, CA 95126

New, used, new-old-stock, reproduction or rebuilt
engines, powerplant parts and so on.

288
Engines and Components, Inc.
12 Lothrop Street
Beverly, MA 01915

New, used, new-old-stock, reproduction or rebuilt
engines, powerplant parts and so on, and high-
performance parts and services.

289
Engine Service Group
Box 13053
Department HMN3
Lansing, MI 48901

New, used, new-old-stock, reproduction or rebuilt
engines, powerplant parts and so on.
Catalog, $2.00.

290
Ericksons Auto Trim & Upholstery
3411 South Center
Sioux Falls, SD 57105

Interior fabric, hardware and trim.

291
Experi-Metal Inc
6345 Wall Street
Sterling Heights, MI 48077

New, used, new-old-stock, reproduction or rebuilt
body and body trim parts.
Free brochure.

292
Faxon's
1655 East 6th Street
Corona, CA 91719

Manuals, parts books, price books, catalogs and
other literature.

293
The Fiberglass Shop
631 North Addison Avenue
Villa Park, IL 60181

New, used, new-old-stock, reproduction or rebuilt
body and body trim parts.

294
Fiberglass and Wood Company
Route 3, Box 800
Nashville, GA 31639

New, used, new-old-stock or reproduction parts and
services.
All 1911-54 models of cars and trucks, excluding
Corvettes.
New, used, new-old-stock, reproduction or rebuilt
body and body trim parts.
Catalog, $3.00.

295
Fifth Avenue Antique Auto Parts
502 Arthur Avenue
Clay Center, KS 67432

New, used, new-old-stock or reproduction vintage
cosmetic and mechanical accessories; new, used,
new-old-stock, reproduction or rebuilt vintage
high-performance parts and services.
All models and eras.
Catalog, $3.00.

296
58 Impalas Limited
Box 406
Medfield, MA 02052

Parts and services.
Full-sized models (i.e., BelAirs, Biscaynes, Caprices,
Impalas, station wagons and so on).

297
The Filling Station
6929 Power Inn Road
Sacramento, CA 95828

New, used, new-old-stock or reproduction parts and
services.
All 1911–54 models of cars and trucks, excluding
Corvettes.
New, used, new-old-stock or reproduction cosmetic
and mechanical accessories; mechanical parts,
body parts, interior parts, trim, chrome, electrical
parts, hardware and other general parts; new,
used, new-old-stock, reproduction or rebuilt
vintage high-performance parts and services.
All models and eras.
Catalog, $4.00.

298
First Generation Camaro
107 Moon Drive
Smithfield, VA 23430

New, used, new-old-stock, reproduction or rebuilt
parts and services.
Camaros from 1967 to present.

299
Five Points
7471 Slater G.
Huntington Beach, CA 92647

New, used, new-old-stock, reproduction or rebuilt
suspension parts, supplies and services.

300
Florida Precision Calipers, Inc.
15711 Tangelo Terrace
Delray Beach, FL 33444

New, used, new-old-stock, reproduction or rebuilt
brake parts.
Corvettes and Camaros.
Free brochure.

301
Forever Classic Chevy Club
Pomona, CA 91766

Restoration, preservation and collection.
Any model.

302
Fort Wayne Clutch
2424 Goshen Road
Fort Wayne, IN 46808

New, used, new-old-stock, reproduction or rebuilt
    transmissions or parts.

303
The Four M Enterprises
10632 Fora Street NW, Suite CC
Minneapolis, MN 55433

Mechanical parts, accessories, body parts, interior
    parts, trim, chrome, electrical parts, hardware
    and other general parts.
All models, all years.
Catalog, $1.00.

304
Four Star Classic Autos
3807 Deats Road
Dickinson, TX 77539

Rebuilding, reconditioning, fabrication or restora-
    tion services; automobile transportation.

305
Four States Motors
Kevil, KY 42053

Mechanical parts, accessories, body parts, interior
    parts, trim, chrome, electrical parts, hardware
    and other general parts.
All models, all years.

306
Francis Burley
Route 7, P.O. Box 1281
Moultrie, GA 31776

Manuals, parts books, price books, catalogs and
other literature.

307
Frank Zoellner
133 South 4th Avenue
Beech Grove, IN 46107

Chrome, cadmium and silver plating; metal polishing; and so on.

308
Free List Publications
Box 3143
Laurel, MD 20708

Manuals, parts books, price books, catalogs and
other literature.

309
Fun Trucking
P.O. Box 24458
Phoenix, AZ 85074

New, used, new-old-stock, reproduction or rebuilt
parts and services.
Pickups and trucks, all years.
New, used, new-old-stock or reproduction cosmetic
and mechanical accessories.
All models and eras.
Catalog, $3.00.

310
Gale Smyth
8316 East AJ Highway
Whitesburg, TN 37891

New, used, new-old-stock, reproduction or rebuilt
body and body trim parts; rechromed bumpers.

311
Garland Radio
3801 Southwest 28 Place
Des Moines, IA 50321

Sales and repair of new, new-old-stock,
    reproduction or rebuilt radios, speakers and
    boosters.

312
Gary's Plastic Chrome Plating
39312 Dillingham
Westland, MI 48185

Chrome, cadmium and silver plating; metal
    polishing; and so on.
Dealer inquiries welcome.

313
Gasket King Company, Limited
18 Hastings Avenue
Toronto, Ontario, Canada M4L 2L2

New, new-old-stock or reproduction automotive
    gaskets.
All models and years.

314
Gateway Reproductions
370 Jungermann Road
Saint Peters, MO 63376

New, used, new-old-stock, reproduction or rebuilt
    parts and services.
Camaros from 1967 to present; Chevelles, El
    Caminos and Malibus from 1964 to present.

315
Gaurdjian Battery Company
Route 1, Box 68
Union City, PA 16438

New, used, new-old-stock, reproduction or rebuilt
    electrical system parts and services (i.e., batteries,
    wiring kits and so on).

316
Generator Exchange
555 1st Street
San Francisco, CA 94107

New, used, new-old-stock, reproduction or rebuilt
electrical system parts and services (i.e., batteries,
wiring kits and so on).

317
Gentile III
5408 Buyers Circle West
Columbus, OH 43229

New, used, new-old-stock, reproduction or rebuilt
parts and services.
Corvettes, all years.

318
George Zaha
615 Elizabeth
Rochester, MI 48063

Sales and repair of new, new-old-stock,
reproduction or rebuilt radios, speakers and
boosters.

319
Gerald Phillips
5101 Mockingbird Road
Greensboro, NC 27406

Fender skirts and visors.
Pickups and trucks.
Free catalog.

320
G. John McGinnis Chevy Auto Parts
3415 Sturbridge Road
Grand Blanc, MI 48439

New, used, new-old-stock or reproduction parts and
services.
All 1955–57 models, excluding Corvettes.
Free catalog.

321
GLASCO
69 Industrial Park Road East
Tolland, CT 06084

New, new-old-stock or reproduction windows,
    windshields and other glass parts.
All models and years.
Send SASE for catalog.

322
Glass Act Corvettes
1012 Manorwood Drive
Logansport, IN 46947

New, used, new-old-stock, reproduction or rebuilt
    parts and services.
Corvettes, all years.

323
GM Hardware and Parts
P.O. Box 80
Macedonia, OH 44056

New, new-old-stock or reproduction trim sources,
    bolts, fasteners and miscellaneous hardware.
Any model.
Catalog, $1.00.

324
GM Muscle Car Parts, Inc.
9748 Utica
Department 27
Evergreen Park, IL 60642

Mechanical parts, accessories, body parts, interior
    parts, trim, chrome, electrical parts, hardware
    and other general parts.
All models, all years.

325
Golden State Pickup Parts
618 East Gutierrez Street
Department HMN
Santa Barbara, CA 93103

5970 Dale Street
Buena Park, CA 90621

New, used, new-old-stock, reproduction or rebuilt
parts and services.
Pickups and trucks, all years.
1947–54 Catalog, $3.00; 1955–66 Builder's Guide and
Catalog, $8.95; 1967–72 Catalog, $3.00.

326
Gomez/World Express, Inc.
55 American Highway
Revere, MA 02151

Automobile transportation.

327
Grady Cox
Route 1, Box 6
Avery, TX 75554

New, used, new-old-stock or reproduction parts and
services.
All 1911–54 models of cars and trucks, excluding
Corvettes.
Free list.

328
Graves Plating
Industrial Park, Highway 17
P.O. Box 1052 HR
Florence, AL 35630

Chrome, cadmium and silver plating; metal
polishing; and so on.

329
Great American Station Wagon Owner's Association
2017 Manatee Avenue West
Bradenton, FL 34205

Restoration, preservation and collection.
Any model.

330

Grey Hills Auto Restoration
P.O. Box 680
Blairstown, NJ 07825

Automobile restoration services.
Any model.

331

Greenhoes Corvette Supplies
5681 Pearl Road
Karma, OH 44129

New, used, new-old-stock, reproduction or rebuilt
parts and services.
Corvettes, 1968–72.

332

Green Mountain Parts
Route 22A
Orwell, VT 05760-9999

New, used, new-old-stock or reproduction parts and
services.
All 1911–54 models of cars and trucks, excluding
Corvettes.
Send SASE; specify model and year.

333

Grossmueller
55 Wolf Hill Drive
Warren, NJ 07060

New, used, new-old-stock, reproduction or rebuilt
parts and services.
Corvettes, all years.

334

Hampton Coach
70 High Street
Box 665
Hampton, NH 03842

Interior fabric, hardware and trim.
Free catalog.

335
Hampton's
P.O. Box 234
2846 Hitchcock
Downers Grove, IL 60515

Interior fabric, hardware and trim; decals and
    stencils for restoration purposes.
Free catalog.

336
Hanlon Plating Company
925 East 4th Street
Richmond, VA 23224

Chrome, cadmium and silver plating; metal
    polishing; and so on.

337
Harkin Machine Shop
115 1st Avenue NW
Watertown, SD 57201

Rebabbitting; new, used, new-old-stock,
    reproduction or rebuilt engines, powerplant parts
    and so on.

338
Harmon's
Highway 27 North, P.O. Box 6A
Geneva, IN 46740

Centerpoint Mall
2655–B Saviers Road
Oxnard, CA 93033

Mechanical parts, accessories, body parts, interior
    parts, trim, chrome, electrical parts, hardware
    and other general parts.
All models, 1955–72.
Catalog, $2.00.

339
Harnesses Unlimited
Box 435
Wayne, PA 19087

New, used, new-old-stock, reproduction or rebuilt
electrical system parts and services (i.e., batteries,
wiring kits and so on).
Catalog, $2.00.

340
Harty's Antique Auto Parts
P.O. Box 43, Old Route 1
Sandy Point, ME 04972

Mechanical parts, accessories, body parts, interior
parts, trim, chrome, electrical parts, hardware
and other general parts; rebuilding,
reconditioning, fabrication or restoration services.
All models, all years.

341
Heavy Chevy Pickup Parts
P.O. Box 650
Department CV
Siloam Springs, AR 72761

New, used, new-old-stock, reproduction or rebuilt
parts and services.
Pickups and trucks, all years.
Catalog, $3.00.

342
Herbert Cams
1933 South Manchester
Anaheim, CA 92802

Camshafts reground to original specifications.

343
Herb Rubin
5806 Southwest 25th Street
Hollywood, FL 33023

New, used, new-old-stock, reproduction or rebuilt
parts and services.
Convertibles, all years.

344
H&H Automotive Electrical
4 Clear Creek Court
Simpsonville, SC 29681

New, used, new-old-stock, reproduction or rebuilt
    parts and services.
Corvettes, all years.
New, used, new-old-stock, reproduction or rebuilt
    electrical system parts and services (i.e., batteries,
    wiring kits and so on).

345
Hibernia Auto Restorations
Maple Terrace
Hibernia, NJ 07842

Rebuilding, reconditioning, fabrication or
    restoration services.

346
High-Speed Salvage
135 Old Northport Road
Kings Park, NY 11754

Block, head and manifold repair.

347
Hills Corvette Service
Star Route 78, P.O. Box 92
Lewisville, OH 43754

New, used, new-old-stock, reproduction or rebuilt
    parts and services.
Corvettes, all years.
Location, purchasing, selling and trading of cars
    and parts.
All models.

348
Hirlinger Chevrolet
State Road 52N, Box 215
Harrison, OH 45030

GM dealers.

Restoration and preservation services; new, new-old-stock, reproduction and rebuilt parts and services; mechanical parts, accessories, body parts, interior parts, trim, chrome, electrical parts, hardware and other general parts.
All models, all years.

349
Hobart Auto
Box K, Route 10, Main Street
Hobart, NY 13788

Rebuilding, reconditioning, fabrication or restoration services.

350
Holt Auto Sales
2253 North Cedar Street
Holt, MI 48842

Location, purchasing, selling and trading of cars and parts.
All models.

351
Hoosier Distributing
3009 West Sample Street
South Bend, IN 46619

Special tools and machinery for restoration and preservation.
Catalog, $2.00.

352
Horseless Carriage Carriers, Inc.
61 Iowa Avenue
Paterson, NJ 07503

Automobile transportation.

353
House of Hubcaps
P.O. Box 6882
Great Falls, MT 59406

New, used, new-old-stock, reproduction or rebuilt
parts and services.
Pickups and trucks, all years.
Wheels and wheel accessories.
All models.

354
House of Powder, Inc.
Route 71 and 1st Street
Box 336
Standard, IL 61363

Powder coating; chrome, cadmium and silver
plating; metal polishing; and so on.

355
Howard Dobuck Chevrolet Parts
5948 West Park Avenue
Cicero, IL 60650

New, used, new-old-stock or reproduction parts and
services.
All 1955–57 models, excluding Corvettes.
Parts and services.
Full-sized 1958–64 models (i.e., BelAirs, Biscaynes,
Caprices, Impalas, station wagons and so on).
Mechanical parts, accessories, body parts, interior
parts, trim, chrome, electrical parts, hardware
and other general parts.
All models, all years.

356
Hubcap Heaven
Route 9
Berwick, ME 03901

Wheels and wheel accessories.
All models.

357
Hydro-E-Lectric
48 Appleton
Auburn, MA 01501

New, used, new-old-stock, reproduction or rebuilt
   parts and services.
Convertibles, all years.

358
Hyperformance Technology
2104 Hillshire Creek
Memphis, TN 38134

Economy and high-performance computer chips.
Late-model automobiles and trucks.

359
Ikerd's Corvettes, Inc.
Route 12, Box 437
Bedford, IN 47421

New, used, new-old-stock, reproduction or rebuilt
   parts and services.
Corvettes, all years.

360
Image Autos
1055 Northeast 43rd Court
Fort Lauderdale, FL 33334

Custom wood graining.

361
Independent Automotive Restorations
454 Lopus Road
Beacon Falls, CT 06403

Rebuilding, reconditioning, fabrication or
   restoration services.

362
Ingersoll-Rand
P.O. Box 7445
Denver, CO 80207

Special tools and machinery for restoration and
   preservation.

363

Instrument Services, Inc.
433 South Arch Street
Janesville, WI 53545

Sales and repair of new, used, new-old-stock,
    reproduction or rebuilt clocks and gauges.

364

Inter Coach Products
624 Valley Street
Lewistown, PA 17044

Interior fabric, hardware and trim.
Catalog, $3.00.

365

Interior Wood Designs
416 Saxonburg Road
Pittsburgh, PA 15238

Cosmetic wood trim and interior body framing.

366

International Camaro Club, Inc.
National Headquarters
2001 Pittston Avenue
Scranton, PA 18505

Restoration, preservation and collection.
Any model.

367

International Registry of Early Corvettes
P.O. Box 666
Corvallis, OR 97339

New, used, new-old-stock, reproduction or rebuilt
    parts and services.
1953–55 Corvettes.

368

International Registry of Salvageable Autos
5141 Sidney Road
Cincinnati, OH 45238

Location, purchasing, selling and trading of cars
and parts.
All models.

369
Iowa Glass Depot
308 6th Avenue SE
Cedar Rapids, IA 52401

New, new-old-stock or reproduction windows,
windshields and other glass parts.
All models and years.

370
Jack H. Bunton
North 604 Freya
Spokane, WA 99202

Camshafts reground to original specifications, and
rebabbitting.

371
Jack Podell
106 Wakewa Avenue
South Bend, IN 46617

New, new-old-stock, reproduction or rebuilt
Rochester fuel injection parts and services.
1957–65.

372
Jack Shaymow Vintique Electronics
52–C Tilford
Deerfield Beach, FL 19934

Sales and repair of new, new-old-stock,
reproduction or rebuilt radios, speakers and
boosters.

373
Jack Turpin
Route 2, Peaceful Valley, Box 2474
Cleveland, GA 30528

Steering wheel restoration.

374

James Erickson
875 West 17th, Unit 1
Costa Mesa, CA 92627

Steering wheel restoration.

375

James Hinshaw
100 Bell Street
Burlington, NC 27215

New, used, new-old-stock, reproduction or rebuilt
parts and services.
Chevelles, El Caminos and Malibus from 1964 to
present; Monte Carlos from 1970 to present.
Catalog, $2.00.

376

James Martin
43 Bowdin Street
Newton Highland, MA 02161

Appraisals and estimates.
All models and eras.

377

James McConville
4205 West 129th Street #22
Hawthorne, CA 90250

New, used, new-old-stock or reproduction parts and
services.
All 1911–54 models of cars and trucks, excluding
Corvettes.

378

James Price
Route 1, Box 1435
Bumpass, VA 23024

Fiberglass tops.
Catalog, $2.00.

379
James Ragsdale
93 Whippany Road
Morristown, NJ 07960

New, used, new-old-stock, reproduction or rebuilt
brake parts, engines, powerplant parts and so on,
and suspension parts, supplies and services.

380
Jayson
545 West Broadway #112
Mesa, AZ 85202

New, used, new-old-stock, reproduction or rebuilt
parts and services.
Convertibles, all years.

381
JC Whitney and Company
1917–19 Archer Avenue
P.O. Box 8410
Chicago, IL 60680

New, used, new-old-stock or reproduction cosmetic
and mechanical accessories; mechanical parts,
body parts, interior parts, trim, chrome, electrical
parts, hardware and other general parts.
All models, all years.

382
J. DeChristopher
Box 148
Feasterville, PA 19047

New, used, new-old-stock, reproduction or rebuilt
suspension parts, supplies and services.

383
Jed Scott Auto Parts
711 Mountain Avenue
Springfield, NJ 07081

Mechanical parts, accessories, body parts, interior
parts, trim, chrome, electrical parts, hardware

and other general parts.
All models, all years.

384
Jeff's Customs
5432 Royal Palm
Tucson, AZ 85705

New, used, new-old-stock or reproduction cosmetic
and mechanical accessories; Continental kits.
All models and eras.

385
J Haugen
871 Shadowgrove
Brea, CA 92621

Mechanical parts, accessories, body parts, interior
parts, trim, chrome, electrical parts, hardware
and other general parts.
All models from 1955 to present.

386
Jim Alexandro
Box 144
Maspeth, NY 11378

New, new-old-stock, reproduction or rebuilt fuel
system parts and services.

387
Jim Carter
1500 East Alton, Unit CB
Independence, MO 64055

New, used, new-old-stock, reproduction or rebuilt
parts and services.
Pickups and trucks, all years.
Catalog, $.75.

388
Jim Glass Corvette Specialists, Inc.
Route 32N
Kingston, NY 12401

New, used, new-old-stock, reproduction or rebuilt
parts and services.
Corvettes from 1963 to present.

389
Jim Osborn Reproductions, Inc.
101-A Ridgecrest Drive
Lawrenceville, GA 30245

Decals and stencils for restoration purposes.
Catalog, $2.00.

390
J&J Corvette Center, Inc.
Highway 63 North
Hudson, IA 50643

New, used, new-old-stock, reproduction or rebuilt
parts and services.
Corvettes, all years.

391
J&J Enterprises
102 A Wheeler Avenue
Collinsville, VA 24078

New, used, new-old-stock, reproduction or rebuilt
parts and services.
Camaros from 1967 to present.
Catalog, $2.00.

392
J&M Auto Parts
Route 5, Box 170
Pelham, NH 03076

Mechanical parts, accessories, body parts, interior
parts, trim, chrome, electrical parts, hardware
and other general parts.
All models, 1955–72.
Catalog, $1.00; specify make and model.

393
Joe Grom
Route 3, Box 212
Taylorsville, KY 40071

New, used, new-old-stock, reproduction or rebuilt
   parts and services.
Novas and Chevy IIs from 1962 to present.

394
Joe Spina
Box 405
Farmingdale, NY 11735

New, new-old-stock or reproduction windows,
   windshields and other glass parts.
All models and years.

395
John Carlson
241 Brandywine Drive
Shrewsbury, MA 01545

Instrument refacing.

396
John Chamber's Chevrolet
P.O. Box 35068
Department SC
Phoenix, AZ 85069

New, used, new-old-stock or reproduction parts and
   services.
All 1955–57 models, excluding Corvettes.
Free catalog.

397
John Dano's Enterprises, Inc.
1170 D. W. Highway
Hooksett, NH 03106

Location, purchasing, selling and trading of cars
   and parts; rebuilding, reconditioning, fabrication
   or restoration services.
All models.

398
John Fern
Route 1, Box 205
Glenville, NE 68941

New, used, new-old-stock, reproduction or rebuilt
body and body trim parts; mechanical parts,
accessories, body parts, interior parts, trim,
chrome, electrical parts, hardware and other
general parts.
All models, all years.

399
John Golden
Route 5, Box 170
Pelham, NH 03076

New, used, new-old-stock, reproduction or rebuilt
parts and services.
Chevelles, El Caminos and Malibus from 1964 to
present.

400
John Kepich
P.O. Box 1365
7520 Clover, Unit 6
Mentor, OH 44060

New, new-old-stock or reproduction exhaust parts
or complete systems.

401
John Kilgore Turbos
718 Jamestown Road
Burbank, CA 91504

New, used, new-old-stock, reproduction or rebuilt
transmissions or parts.
Catalog, $1.00.

402
Johns Automotive
Route 22
Cambridge, NY 12816

New, used, new-old-stock, reproduction or rebuilt
parts and services.
Corvettes, all years.

403
John's Corvette Care
23954 Kean Street
Dearborn, MI 48124

New, used, new-old-stock, reproduction or rebuilt
    parts and services.
Corvettes, all years.
Catalog, $3.00.

404
Johns NOS Monte Carlo Parts
P.O. Box 1445
Salem, NH 03079

New, used, new-old-stock, reproduction or rebuilt
    parts and services.
Chevelles, El Caminos and Malibus from 1964 to
    present; Monte Carlos from 1970 to present.
Catalog, $1.00.

405
John Tosy
714 South Street
Wrentham, MA 02093

Steering wheel restoration.

406
John Wolf and Company
4550 Wood Street
Willoughby, OH 44094

Sales and repair of new, used, new-old-stock,
    reproduction or rebuilt clocks and gauges.

407
Jon W. Gateman and Son
Route 4, Box 780
Vashow, WA 98070

Gauge refinishing.

408
JR's Fiberglass
J. R. Stafford
1700 Debbie Lane
Statesville, NC 28677

Fiberglass replacements; new, used, new-old-stock,
   reproduction or rebuilt body and body trim parts.

409
Just Dashes, Inc.
5945 Hazeltine Avenue
Van Nuys, CA 91401

Dash pads and overlays.

410
Just Suspension
P.O. Box 167
Towaco, NJ 07082

New, used, new-old-stock, reproduction or rebuilt
   suspension parts, supplies and services.

411
J&W
Route 1, Box 1600
Cascade, VA 24069

New, used, new-old-stock, reproduction or rebuilt
   parts and services.
Novas and Chevy IIs from 1962 to present.
Free catalog.

412
Kaleidoscope
Box 86–11
Mount Ephraim, NJ 08059

Windshield scratch and chip removal.

413
Kalmus Classics
1331 South Dixie Highway West, Unit 10A
Pompano Beach, FL 33060

Mechanical parts, accessories, body parts, interior
parts, trim, chrome, electrical parts, hardware
and other general parts.
All models, 1955–72.
Free catalog.

414
Kanter Auto Products
76 Monroe Street
Boonton, NJ 07005

New, used, new-old-stock, reproduction or rebuilt
brake parts, engines, powerplant parts and so on,
and suspension parts, supplies and services.
Free catalog.

415
Kastelic Vintage Parts
Box 245
Verona, PA 15147

New, used, new-old-stock or reproduction parts and
services.
All 1911–54 models of cars and trucks, excluding
Corvettes.

416
Keen Vette
9850 Cilley Road
Cleves, OH 45002

New, used, new-old-stock, reproduction or rebuilt
parts and services.
Corvettes, all years.

417
Kelly's
P.O. Box 429
Doerun, GA 31744

Manuals, parts books, price books, catalogs and
other literature.

418
Kenask Spring Company
301–307 Manhattan Avenue
Jersey City, NJ 07307

New, used, new-old-stock, reproduction or rebuilt
    suspension parts, supplies and services.

419
Ken McGee
232 Britannia Road West
Goderich, Ontario, Canada N7A 2B9

Manuals, parts books, price books, catalogs and
    other literature.
Send SASE for catalog.

420
Kent-Moore Allied Division, Sealed Power
    Corporation
Department SC
29784 Little Mack
Roseville, MI 48066

Special tools and machinery for restoration and
    preservation.

421
Ken Unger
1327 South Polley Ann
Tempe, AZ 85281

Parts and services.
1958 full-sized models (i.e., BelAirs, Biscaynes,
    Caprices, Impalas, station wagons and so on).
Send SASE for catalog.

422
Keystone Chevelle Club
653 Troch Road
Bath, PA 18014

Restoration, preservation and collection.
Any model.

423
KIA Photography
453H Main
Nashua, NH 03060

Automotive business cards and sales aids.
Samples, $1.00.

424
King's Restoration
2102 Lukens Street NW
Roanoke, VA 24012

Rebuilding, reconditioning, fabrication or
    restoration services.

425
KIRT
437 W McCarty Street
Indianapolis, IN 46225

New, used, new-old-stock, reproduction or rebuilt
    cooling system parts and services.

426
K&R Restorations
1345 Hidden Springs Lane
Glendora, CA 91740

Porcelainizing; chrome, cadmium and silver plating;
    metal polishing; and so on.

427
Lafferty & Associates Auto Transport Company
11506 North Virginia
Kansas City, MO 64155

Automobile transportation.

428
La Riche Corvette Parts/Chevrolet
215 East Main Cross Street
Findlay, OH 45840

GM dealers.
Restoration and preservation services; new, new-
    old-stock, reproduction and rebuilt parts and
    services.

New, used, new-old-stock, reproduction or rebuilt
parts and services.
Corvettes, all years.
Mechanical parts, accessories, body parts, interior
parts, trim, chrome, electrical parts, hardware
and other general parts.
All models.

429
Larry Fischer
180 West 19th Street
Huntington Station, NY 11746

New, used, new-old-stock, reproduction or rebuilt
transmissions or parts.
Free catalog.

430
Larry Thomas
P.O. Box 4
Goshen, OH 45122

New, used, new-old-stock, reproduction or rebuilt
parts and services.
Corvairs, all years.

431
Late Great Chevies
P.O. Box 17824
Orlando, FL 32860

Restoration, preservation and collection.
Any model of 1958–64 full-sized Chevrolet.

432
Lawrence Camuso
219 South 20th Street
San Jose, CA 95116

New, used, new-old-stock, reproduction or rebuilt
body and body trim parts.

433
LCVA
Route 14, Box 468
Jonesborough, TN 37659

Restoration, preservation and collection.
Any model of pickup and truck.
Send SASE for catalog.

434
Lee's Classic Chevy
314 Main
Glenbeulah, WI 53023

New, used, new-old-stock or reproduction parts and
    services.
All 1955–57 models, excluding Corvettes.
Send SASE for catalog.

435
Legendary Corvette, Inc.
903 Eason Road
Warrington, PA 18976

New, used, new-old-stock, reproduction or rebuilt
    parts and services.
Corvettes, all years.
New, used, new-old-stock, reproduction or rebuilt
    body and body trim parts; interior fabric,
    hardware and trim.

436
L&L Antique Auto Trim
403 Spruce
P.O. Box 1177
Pierce City, MO 65723

Interior fabric, hardware and trim.

437
Lloyd's Literature
Box 491
Newbury, OH 44065

Manuals, parts books, price books, catalogs and
other literature.
Send SASE for catalog.

438
Lomotion Corvette Sales
Route 55
Poughkeepsie, NY 12600

New, used, new-old-stock, reproduction or rebuilt
parts and services.
Corvettes, all years.
Location, purchasing, selling and trading of cars
and parts.
All models.

439
Long Island Corvette Supply, Inc.
415 Bayview Avenue
Amityville, NY 11701

New, used, new-old-stock, reproduction or rebuilt
parts and services.
Corvettes, all years.
Catalog, $3.00.

440
Lowell Kimball
810 Prospect Avenue
Norfolk, NE 68701

New, used, new-old-stock or reproduction parts and
services.
All 1911-54 models of cars and trucks, excluding
Corvettes.

441
L. Williams
P.O. Box 3307
Palmer, PA 18043

New, used, new-old-stock, reproduction or rebuilt
parts and services.
1956-57 Corvettes.
Free catalog.

442
Magnum Automotive Products
13578 Pumice Street
Department HM
Norwalk, CA 90650

New, used, new-old-stock, reproduction or rebuilt
    parts and services.
Chevelles, El Caminos and Malibus from 1964 to
    present.
Catalog, $3.00.

443
Marcel's Corvette Shop
Route 4 and 32
Mechanicville, NY 12118

New, used, new-old-stock, reproduction or rebuilt
    parts and services.
Corvettes, all years.

444
Mark Rubin
931 Yale Street
Santa Monica, CA 90403

New, used, new-old-stock, reproduction or rebuilt
    parts and services.
Camaros from 1967 to present.

445
Mar-K Specialized Manufacturing Company
8022 North Wilshire Court
Oklahoma City, OK 73132

New, used, new-old-stock or reproduction cosmetic
    and mechanical accessories.
All models and eras.
New, used, new-old-stock, reproduction or rebuilt
    parts and services.
Pickups and trucks, all years.
Free catalog.

100

446

Mark Wallach, Limited
27 New Street
Nyack-on-Hudson, NY 10960

Rebuilding, reconditioning, fabrication or
restoration services.

447

Martin's of Philadelphia
7327 State Road
Philadelphia, PA 19136

Chrome, cadmium and silver plating; metal
polishing; and so on.

448

Martz Classic Chevy Parts
Route 1, Box 199B
Thomasville, PA 17364

Mechanical parts, accessories, body parts, interior
parts, trim, chrome, electrical parts, hardware
and other general parts.
All models, 1954–72.
Catalog, $1.00.

449

Marvin Roth Antique Radios
14500 Labelle
Oak Park, MI 48237

Sales and repair of new, new-old-stock,
reproduction or rebuilt radios, speakers and
boosters.

450

M. C. Productions, Inc.
8686 East M-115
Cadillac, MI 49601

Mechanical parts, accessories, body parts, interior
parts, trim, chrome, electrical parts, hardware
and other general parts.
All models, all years.

451
Melrose T-Top International
655 Central, Unit F
Wooddale, IL 60191

Factory replacement and custom T-top parts and
   services.

452
Metalcraft
P.O. Box 925
Iowa City, IA 52242

Aluminum panels.

453
Metro Moulded Parts, Inc.
Department A
11610 Jay Street
P.O. Box 33130
Minneapolis, MN 55433

New, new-old-stock or reproduction weather
   stripping, moldings, gaskets, seals and other
   rubber parts.
Catalog, $2.00.

454
M. F. Dobbins
3045 Pennypack Road
Hatboro, PA 19040

New, used, new-old-stock, reproduction or rebuilt
   parts and services.
Corvettes, all years.
Mechanical parts, accessories, body parts, interior
   parts, trim, chrome, electrical parts, hardware
   and other general parts.
All models, all years.

455
M&H Electric Fabricators
5413 Cortland Avenue
Lynwood, CA 90262

New, used, new-old-stock, reproduction or rebuilt
electrical system parts and services (i.e., batteries,
wiring kits and so on).

456
Mid-America Promotions
P.O. Box 256
Willow Springs, IL 60480

Location, purchasing, selling and trading of cars
and parts.
All models.

457
Midbank
6563 Worthington-Galena Road
Worthington, OH 43085

Classic and antique auto financing.

458
Midsouth Speedometer
1633 Midland Boulevard
Fort Smith, AR 72901

Sales and repair of new, used, new-old-stock,
reproduction or rebuilt clocks and gauges.

459
Mike Drago Chevrolet Parts
141 East Saint Joseph Street
Easton, PA 18042

New, used, new-old-stock or reproduction parts and
services.
All 1955–57 models, excluding Corvettes.

460
Mike Harrington
112 Indian Church Road
West Seneca, NY 14224

Mechanical parts, accessories, body parts, interior
parts, trim, chrome, electrical parts, hardware
and other general parts.
All models, all years.

461
Mike Jones Carburetion
7602 Talbert Avenue
Huntington Beach, CA 92648

New, new-old-stock, reproduction or rebuilt fuel
system parts and services.
Brochure, $2.00.

462
Mike Lawson
59 Leader Drive
Jacobus, PA 17407

New, used, new-old-stock, reproduction or rebuilt
parts and services.
Convertibles, all years.

463
Mike Rollins Restorations
P.O. Box 877
Canadian, TX 79014

Mechanical parts, accessories, body parts, interior
parts, trim, chrome, electrical parts, hardware
and other general parts.
All models, all years.

464
Mike's
7716 Deering Avenue
Canoga Park, CA 91304

Mechanical parts, accessories, body parts, interior
parts, trim, chrome, electrical parts, hardware
and other general parts.
All models, 1955–72.
Dealer inquiries welcome.

465
Mike Walker's Camaros Unlimited
1008 South Main
Searcy, AR 72143

New, used, new-old-stock, reproduction or rebuilt
parts and services.
Camaros from 1967 to present.

466
Mill Supply
Department PS-609
3241 Superior Avenue
Cleveland, OH 44114

New, used, new-old-stock, reproduction or rebuilt
body and body trim parts.
Catalog, $3.00.

467
Modern Performance Classics
4321 East Chapman Avenue
Orange, CA 92669

New, used, new-old-stock, reproduction or rebuilt
parts and services.
Novas and Chevy IIs from 1962 to present.

468
Mo-Ma Manufacturing
10853 Magnolia
North Hollywood, CA 91601

Sales and repair of new, used, new-old-stock,
reproduction or rebuilt clocks and gauges.

469
Mooney's Antique Auto Parts
Star Route, Box 645C, Highway 59N
Goodrich, TX 77335

New, used, new-old-stock or reproduction parts and
services.
All 1911–54 models of cars and trucks, excluding
Corvettes.
Free catalog.

470

The Motion Picture Vehicle Owners Club
304 Newbury Street, Suite 24D
Boston, MA 02115

Restoration, preservation and collection.
Models used in motion pictures.

471

Motorite
1530 East Washington
Louisville, KY 40206

New, used, new-old-stock, reproduction or rebuilt
    engines, powerplant parts and so on.
Catalog, $1.00.

472

M Parker Autoworks
510 Walnut Avenue
Laurel Springs, NJ 08021

New, used, new-old-stock, reproduction or rebuilt
    electrical system parts and services (i.e., batteries,
    wiring kits and so on).
Dealer inquiries welcome.

473

Mr. G's Rechromed Plastic
5613 Elliot Reeder Road
Fort Worth, TX 76117

Chrome, cadmium and silver plating; metal
    polishing; and so on.

474

Mr. Nomad
615 North Jenifer
East Wenatchee, WA 98801

New, used, new-old-stock or reproduction parts and
    services.
All 1955–57 models, excluding Corvettes.
Catalog, $4.00.

475
Mr. Smog
1804 Ogden
Downers Grove, IL 60515

Factory emission control equipment, parts and
services.

476
Mr. Suspension
P.O. Box 396
Montville, NJ 07045

New, used, new-old-stock, reproduction or rebuilt
suspension parts, supplies and services.

477
Mr. Machinist/Model Maker
15348 Falmouth
Houston, TX 77001

New, used, new-old-stock, reproduction or rebuilt
348/409 engines, powerplant parts and so on.

478
Muscle Cars Only
Route 1, Box 221
Hunker, PA 15639

Mechanical parts, accessories, body parts, interior
parts, trim, chrome, electrical parts, hardware
and other general parts.
All models, all years.
Catalog, $2.00.

479
Musclecar Specialties
Box 140-K
1450 Johnston Road
White Rock, British Columbia, Canada V4B 5E9

Mechanical parts, accessories, body parts, interior
parts, trim, chrome, electrical parts, hardware
and other general parts.
All models, all years.

480
Muscle 'n' More
1055 South Pacific Avenue
Woodburn, OR 97071

Mechanical parts, accessories, body parts, interior
   parts, trim, chrome, electrical parts, hardware
   and other general parts.
All models, all years.

481
Muskegon Brake
848 East Broadway
Muskegon, MI 49444

New, used, new-old-stock, reproduction or rebuilt
   brake parts.

482
National Chevelle Owner's Association
P.O. Box 5014
Department SC
Greensboro, NC 27435-0014

Restoration, preservation and collection.
Any model.

483
National Chevy Association
947 Arcade
Saint Paul, MN 55106

Restoration, preservation and collection.
Any model of 1953–54 Chevrolet.

484
National Council of Corvette Clubs
2219 North 22nd
Saint Joseph, MO 64505

Listing of clubs involved with restoration,
   preservation and collection.
Any model.

485

National Impala Association
Department A
P.O. Box 968
Spearfish, SD 57783

Restoration, preservation and collection.
Any model.

486

National Monte Carlo Owners Association
P.O. Box 187
Independence, KY 41051

Restoration, preservation and collection.
Any model.

487

National Nomad Club
4691 South Mariposa Drive
Englewood, CO 80110

Restoration, preservation and collection.
Any model.

488

National Nostalgic Nova Club
P.O. Box 2344
Department HR
York, PA 17405

Restoration, preservation and collection.
Any model.

489

National Parts Depot
3101 Southwest 40th Boulevard
Gainesville, FL 32601

New, used, new-old-stock, reproduction or rebuilt
    parts and services.
Camaros from 1967 to present.
Free catalog.

490
National Spring Company
630 Grand Avenue
Spring Valley, CA 92077

New, used, new-old-stock, reproduction or rebuilt
  suspension parts, supplies and services.

491
Nationwide Listings, Inc.
2301 Collins Avenue
P.O. Box P
Miami Beach, FL 33139

Location, purchasing, selling and trading of cars
  and parts.
All models.

492
Newcastle Battery Manufacturing Company
P.O. Box 5040
Newcastle, PA 16105

New, used, new-old-stock, reproduction or rebuilt
  electrical system parts and services (i.e., batteries,
  wiring kits and so on).

493
N.E.W. Corvette Supply
6566 Green Bay Road
Sturgeon Bay, WI 54235

New, used, new-old-stock, reproduction or rebuilt
  parts and services.
Corvettes, all years.

494
Newman International Transport
101 East Kennedy Boulevard, Suite 1490
Tampa, FL 33602

Automobile transportation.

495
Nick's Chevy Parts
7505 Delmar
Saint Louis, MO 63130

New, used, new-old-stock or reproduction parts and
   services.
All 1955-57 models, excluding Corvettes.

496
Norm's Antique Auto Supply
1921 Hickory Grove
Davenport, IA 51804

Speedometer and cable repair; new, used, new-old-
   stock, reproduction or rebuilt electrical system
   parts and services (i.e., batteries, wiring kits and
   so on); new, new-old-stock, reproduction or
   rebuilt fuel system parts and services.

497
North American Super Sports
2309 Terrace Drive
Burnsville, MN 55337

Restoration, preservation and collection.
Any model.

498
Northeast Chevy GMC Trucking Club
P.O. Box 135
Millers Falls, MA 01349

Restoration, preservation and collection.
Any model.

499
Northern Auto Parts Warehouse
613 Water Street
Sioux City, IA 51102

Mechanical parts, accessories, body parts, interior
   parts, trim, chrome, electrical parts, hardware
   and other general parts.
All models, all years.

500

Northwestern Auto
1101 South Division
Grand Rapids, MI 49507

New, used, new-old-stock, reproduction or rebuilt
electrical system parts and services (i.e., batteries,
wiring kits and so on); new, new-old-stock,
reproduction or rebuilt fuel system parts and
services.

501

Northwest Modern Classics
121 Duryea
Raymond, WA 98577

Interior fabric, hardware and trim.

502

Northwest Transmission Parts
13500 U.S. Route 62
Winchester, OH 45697

New, used, new-old-stock, reproduction or rebuilt
transmissions or parts.

503

Oak Bows
122 Ramsey Avenue
Chambersburg, PA 17201

Top bows.
New, used, new-old-stock, reproduction or rebuilt
parts and services.
Convertibles, all years.

504

Oakland County Classic Chevy Club
1331 Van Vleet Road
Flushing, MI 48433

Restoration, preservation and collection.
Any model.

505
O. B. Smith Classic Cars and Parts
P.O. Box 11703 HR
Lexington, KY 40577

New, used, new-old-stock or reproduction parts and
services.
All 1955-57 models, excluding Corvettes.
Mechanical parts, accessories, body parts, interior
parts, trim, chrome, electrical parts, hardware
and other general parts.
All models, 1958-72.
Catalog, $1.00.

506
Obsolete Chevy Parts Company, Inc.
524 Hazel Avenue
Department CC
P.O. Box 68
Nashville, GA 31639

Mechanical parts, accessories, body parts, interior
parts, trim, chrome, electrical parts, hardware
and other general parts.
All models, all years.
Catalog, $2.50; specify year and model.

507
Obsolete Parts
131 Broadway
Chula Vista, CA 92010

Mechanical parts, accessories, body parts, interior
parts, trim, chrome, electrical parts, hardware
and other general parts.
All models from 1955 to present.
New, used, new-old-stock, reproduction or rebuilt
parts and services.
Pickups and trucks, all years.
Catalog, $2.50.

508
OEM Glass, Inc.
Box 362, Highway 9 East
Bloomington, IL 61702

New, new-old-stock or reproduction windows,
    windshields and other glass parts.
All models and years.

509
Ohio Auto Paint
350 State Street
Wadsworth, OH 44281

Dipping and stripping.

510
Ohio Valley Street Parts
6041 Harrison Avenue
Department A
Cincinnati, OH 45248

Mechanical parts, accessories, body parts, interior
    parts, trim, chrome, electrical parts, hardware
    and other general parts.
All models, all years.
Catalog, $2.00 per year.

511
OLCAR Bearing Company
5101 Fedora
Troy, MI 48098

New, used, new-old-stock, reproduction or rebuilt
    transmissions or parts.

512
Old Car Parts
Box 184
Clear Lake, IA 50428

New, used, new-old-stock or reproduction parts and
    services.
All 1911-54 models of cars and trucks, excluding
    Corvettes.
Catalog, $3.00.

114

513
Old Car Parts Company
13405 Bryant Avenue South
Burnsville, MN 55337

New, used, new-old-stock, reproduction or rebuilt
body and body trim parts; mechanical parts,
accessories, interior parts, chrome, electrical
parts, hardware and other general parts; new,
new-old-stock or reproduction weather stripping,
moldings, gaskets, seals and other rubber parts.
All models, all years.

514
Old Cars
505 South Tibbs
Indianapolis, IN 46241

New, used, new-old-stock or reproduction parts and
services.
All 1911–54 models of cars and trucks, excluding
Corvettes.

515
Old Car Services
P.O. Box 242
Neshanic Station, NJ 08853

New, used, new-old-stock, reproduction or rebuilt
brake parts and suspension parts, supplies and
services.

517
Old Chevy Trucks
3014 Dedman
Pasadena, TX 77503

New, used, new-old-stock, reproduction or rebuilt
parts and services.
Pickups and trucks, all years.
Free catalog.

518
The Old Coach Works
1206 Badger Street
Yorkville, IL 60560

Rebuilding, reconditioning, fabrication or
restoration services.

519
The Oldie Goldie Shop
Route 1, Box 124
Elm City, NC 27822

New, used, new-old-stock, reproduction or rebuilt
parts and services.
Pickups and trucks, 1947–59.
Catalog, $3.00.

520
Ol' 55
4154 A Skyron Drive
Doylestown, PA 18901

New, used, new-old-stock or reproduction parts and
services.
All 1955–57 models, excluding Corvettes.
Mechanical parts, accessories, body parts, interior
parts, trim, chrome, electrical parts, hardware
and other general parts.
All models, all years.
Catalog, $3.00.

521
Original Auto Interiors
7869 Trumble
Saint Clair, MI 48079

Interior fabric, hardware and trim.

522
Original Parts Company
P.O. Box 949
LaSalle, CO 80645

New, used, new-old-stock or reproduction parts and
services.
All 1911–54 models of cars and trucks, excluding
Corvettes.

523
Ortiz Enterprises
4000 Regatto Road
Yukon, OK 73099

Chrome trim.

524
Out of the Past Parts
3720 Southwest 23rd Street
Gainesville, FL 32601

New, used, new-old-stock or reproduction parts and
services.
All 1911–54 models of cars and trucks, excluding
Corvettes.
Send SASE for catalog.

525
Pacific Corvette
5722 112th Street East
Puyallup, WA 98373

New, used, new-old-stock, reproduction or rebuilt
parts and services.
Corvettes, all years.

526
Packard Farm
97 N/150W
Greenfield, IN 46140

New, used, new-old-stock or reproduction parts and
services.
All 1911–54 models of cars and trucks, excluding
Corvettes.

527
The Paddock, Inc.
221 West Main
Box 30
Department HR
Knightstown, IN 46148

New, used, new-old-stock, reproduction or rebuilt
parts and services.
Camaros from 1967 to present; Chevelles, El
Caminos and Malibus from 1964 to present;
Monte Carlos from 1970 to present; Novas and
Chevy IIs from 1962 to present.
Catalog, $1.00.

528
Paddock West
Department BG
Redlands, CA 92373

New, used, new-old-stock, reproduction or rebuilt
parts and services.
Camaros from 1967 to present; Chevelles, El
Caminos and Malibus from 1964 to present;
Monte Carlos from 1970 to present; Novas and
Chevy IIs from 1962 to present.
Catalog, $1.00.

529
Palm Springs Obsolete Automotive
555 North Commercial Road, Unit 3
Department SC
Palm Springs, CA 92262

Mechanical parts, accessories, body parts, interior
parts, trim, chrome, electrical parts, hardware
and other general parts.
All models, all years.
Catalog, $6.00.

530
Palo Alto Speedometer, Inc.
718 Emerson Street
Palo Alto, CA 94301

Sales and repair of new, used, new-old-stock, reproduction or rebuilt clocks and gauges.

531
PAM Warehouse, Inc.
200 Petro Avenue
Sioux Falls, SD 57100

Mechanical parts, accessories, trim, electrical parts, hardware and other general parts.
All models, all years.

532
Paragon Corvette Reproductions
8040 South Jennings Road
Swartz Creek, MI 48473

New, used, new-old-stock, reproduction or rebuilt parts and services.
Corvettes, all years.

533
Paragon Productions
5796 Wellson Drive
Cypress, CA 90630

Chrome, cadmium and silver plating; metal polishing; and so on.

534
Parts House
2912 Hunter
Fort Worth, TX 76112

New, used, new-old-stock, reproduction or rebuilt engines, powerplant parts and so on.

535
Parts of the Past
Box 602
Waukesha, WI 53187

Manuals, parts books, price books, catalogs and other literature.
Send SASE and specify needs.

536
Parts Unlimited
10 South 123 Norman Town Road
Naperville, IL 60565

New, used, new-old-stock, reproduction or rebuilt
   parts and services.
All models from mid-fifties to present.
Camaros from 1967 to present.

537
Paul's Auto
816 Market Street
Dekalb, IL 60115

Mechanical parts, accessories, body parts, interior
   parts, trim, chrome, electrical parts, hardware
   and other general parts.
All models from 1955 to present.
Free lists.

538
Pauls Chrome Plating, Inc.
Mars-Valencia Road
Mars, PA 16046

Chrome, cadmium and silver plating; metal
   polishing; and so on.

539
Pauls Rod & Bearing
111 North Bridge
Smithville, MO 64089

Rebabbitting and all types of bearings.

540
Perfection Auto Restoration
Route 2, 550 North, 625 West
Hobart, IN 46342

Chrome, cadmium and silver plating; metal
   polishing; and so on.

541
Performance Automotive Wholesale, Inc.
21122 Lassen Street
Chatsworth, CA 91311

New, used, new-old-stock, reproduction or rebuilt
  high-performance parts and services.

542
Performance Poster Company
4 Stewart Court
Denville, NJ 07834

Automotive posters.

543
Pete Rojas
1964 Terrace
Dinuba, CA 93618

Fender skirts.

544
Petty John Auto Electric
742 Boulevard
Athens, GA 30601

New, used, new-old-stock, reproduction or rebuilt
  electrical system parts and services (i.e., batteries,
  wiring kits and so on).

545
Phillip Clark
10245 Southwest 124th Avenue
Miami, FL 33186

New, used, new-old-stock, reproduction or rebuilt
  transmissions or parts.

546
Phillips Classic Auto Glass
8855 Springbrook Road
Rockford, IL 61111

New, new-old-stock or reproduction windows, windshields and other glass parts.
All models and years.

547
Phil Reed's Classic Chevrolet Motor Company
P.O. Box 14398
10520 River Road
Kansas City, MO 64152

Mechanical parts, accessories, body parts, interior
parts, trim, chrome, electrical parts, hardware
and other general parts.
All models, all years.

548
Piper's Corvette Specialties, Inc.
2 North Avenue
Vermilion, IL 61955

New, used, new-old-stock, reproduction or rebuilt
parts and services.
Corvettes, all years.

549
Plating Service
North 3503 Highway 55
Chilton, WI 53014

Chrome, cadmium and silver plating; metal
polishing; and so on.

550
Potmetal Restorations
4794C Woodlane Circle
Tallahassee, FL 32303

Chrome, cadmium and silver plating; metal
polishing; and so on.
Free brochure.

551
Powell Radiator Service
51 North Lincoln
Box 427
Wilmington, OH 45177

New, used, new-old-stock, reproduction or rebuilt
cooling system parts and services.

552
Power Brake
1775 Monterey Road, 40-B
San Jose, CA 95112

Power brake booster restoration.

553
Precision Auto Restoration
5 Folts Road
Herkimer, NY 13350

Mechanical parts, accessories, body parts, interior
    parts, trim, chrome, electrical parts, hardware
    and other general parts.
All models, all years.

554
Precision Engine and Machine
North 8415 Branch Road
Ixonia, WI 53036

New, used, new-old-stock, reproduction or rebuilt
    engines, powerplant parts and so on.

555
Precision Measurement
P.O. Box 28097
San Antonio, TX 78228

Special tools and machinery for restoration and
    preservation.

556
Pro Antique Auto Parts
Department C
50 King Spring Road
Windsor Locks, CT 06096

New, used, new-old-stock or reproduction parts and
    services.
All 1911-57 models of cars and trucks, excluding
    Corvettes; full-sized models (i.e., BelAirs,
    Biscaynes, Caprices, Impalas, station wagons and
    so on).
Catalog, $2.00.

557
Qual Krom, Inc.
28 Orchard Place
Poughkeepsie, NY 12601

Chrome, cadmium and silver plating; metal
polishing; and so on.

558
Quiksilver Chrome Company
644 North Poplar Street, Unit J
Orange, CA 92668

Chrome, cadmium and silver plating; metal
polishing; and so on.

559
Racecars in Retrospect, Inc.
Box 3116
Alliance, OH 44601

New, new-old-stock, reproduction or rebuilt fuel
system parts and services.

560
Racer's Warehouse
P.O. Box 464
Southhaven, MS 38671

New, used, new-old-stock, reproduction or rebuilt
high-performance parts and services.

561
Radiator Express
3595–C South Higuera Street
Department S
San Luis Obispo, CA 93401

New, used, new-old-stock, reproduction or rebuilt
cooling system parts and services.
Catalog, $3.00.

562
Radios and Wheelcovers World
2718 Koper
Sterling Heights, MI 48310

Sales and repair of new, new-old-stock,
reproduction or rebuilt radios, speakers and
boosters; wheels and wheel accessories.
All models.
Send SASE for catalog.

563
The Radio Workshop
128 Pautipang Hill Road
Baltic, CT 06330

Sales and repair of new, new-old-stock,
reproduction or rebuilt radios, speakers and
boosters.

564
Rare Iron Company
1393 Ann Arbor Trail
Plymouth, MI 48170

Mechanical parts, accessories, body parts, interior
parts, trim, chrome, electrical parts, hardware
and other general parts.
All models, all years.

565
Rays Obsolete Chevrolet Parts
Department 49/54
3430 West National Road
Springfield, OH 45504

Mechanical parts, accessories, body parts, interior
parts, trim, chrome, electrical parts, hardware
and other general parts.
All models, all years.

566
Ray's Upholstery
600 Saint Francis Cabrini Avenue
Scranton, PA 18504

Interior fabric, hardware and trim.

567
RBR Electronics
460 East 319th Street
Willowick, OH 44094

New, used, new-old-stock, reproduction or rebuilt
electrical system parts and services (i.e., batteries,
wiring kits and so on).

568
RB's Obsolete Automotive
7130 Bickford Avenue
Snohomish, WA 98290

Mechanical parts, accessories, body parts, interior
parts, trim, chrome, electrical parts, hardware
and other general parts.
All models, all years.
New, used, new-old-stock, reproduction or rebuilt
parts and services.
Pickups and trucks, all years.
Catalog, $4.00.

569
R. Buzz
909 Phoenix Street
Pittsburgh, PA 15220

Chrome, cadmium and silver plating; metal
polishing; and so on.

570
Registry Financial Services of America, Inc.
3000 West Hallandale Beach Boulevard
Hallandale, FL 33009

Classic and antique auto financing.

571
Reproduction Auto Parts
Box 5388
Charleston, WV 25362

Mechanical parts, accessories, body parts, interior
parts, trim, chrome, electrical parts, hardware

and other general parts.
All models, all years.

572
Restoration Auto Parts
East 13116 12th
Spokane, WA 99216

Mechanical parts, accessories, body parts, interior
    parts, trim, chrome, electrical parts, hardware
    and other general parts.
All models, all years.

573
Restoration Battery
3335 Robinet
Cincinnati, OH 45238

New, used, new-old-stock, reproduction or rebuilt
    electrical system parts and services (i.e., batteries,
    wiring kits and so on).

574
Reynolds Head and Block Repair
2632 East 13th Place
Tulsa, OK 74104

Engine block and head repair.

575
Reynolds Speedometer Repair
4 Lobad Drive
Danvers, MA 01923

Sales and repair of new, used, new-old-stock,
    reproduction or rebuilt clocks and gauges.

576
RGR Camaro Specialists
14941 Ramona Boulevard
Baldwin Park, CA 91706

New, used, new-old-stock, reproduction or rebuilt
    parts and services.
Camaros from 1967 to present.

577
Rhode Island Wiring Service
Box 3737 H
Peace Dale, RI 02883

New, used, new-old-stock, reproduction or rebuilt
electrical system parts and services (i.e., batteries,
wiring kits and so on).
Catalog, $2.00.

578
Rick Shnitzler Original Literature
Box 521
Narberth, PA 19072

Manuals, parts books, price books, catalogs and
other literature.

579
Ridgerunner Auto
P.O. Box 1115
Chadron, NE 69337

Mechanical parts, accessories, body parts, interior
parts, trim, chrome, electrical parts, hardware
and other general parts.
All models, all years.

580
Ridon Pumps
P.O. Box 14142
Pittsburgh, PA 15239

New, used, new-old-stock, reproduction or rebuilt
cooling system parts and services; new, new-old-
stock, reproduction or rebuilt fuel system parts
and services.

581
Rik's Corvette Shoppe
Route 4, Box 778
Morgantown, NC 28655

New, used, new-old-stock, reproduction or rebuilt
parts and services.
Corvettes, all years.
Catalog, $1.00; specify year.

582
R. L. Williams
P.O. Box 3307
Palmer, PA 18043

New, used, new-old-stock, reproduction or rebuilt
   parts and services.
1953–55 Corvettes.
Free catalog.

583
RM Auto Restoration, Limited
825 Park Avenue West
Chatham, Ontario, Canada N7M 5J6

Rebuilding, reconditioning, fabrication or
   restoration services.

584
Road King, Inc.
Route 2, Box 271-A
Yankton, SD 57078

Transport trailers and parts.

585
Robert Heise
11 Bond Street East
Norwalk, CT 06855

Electrical wiring diagrams.
1915–67 models.
Send SASE and specify needs.

586
Robert Lemke
12715 Clinton Street
Alden, NY 14004

Parts and services.
1960–66 full-sized models (i.e., BelAirs, Biscaynes,
   Caprices, Impalas, station wagons and so on).

587
Robert Midland
Box B
Hawley, PA 18428

Mechanical parts, accessories, body parts, interior
   parts, trim, chrome, electrical parts, hardware
   and other general parts.
All models, all years.

588
Roberts Motor Parts
Department HMN
17 Prospect Street
West Newbury, MA 01985

New, used, new-old-stock, reproduction or rebuilt
   parts and services.
Pickups and trucks, all years.
Catalog, $2.00.

589
Robidoux Repair and Sales
1234 South 9th Street
Lincoln, NE 68502

Special tools and machinery for restoration and
   preservation.

590
Rods and Babbitt Machine Works, Inc.
712 East 135th Street
New York, NY 10454

Rebabbitting and connecting rod reconditioning.

591
Rod's Restoration and Parts
12290 North Yorkdale Drive
Baton Rouge, LA 70811

New, used, new-old-stock or reproduction parts and
   services.
All 1955–57 models, excluding Corvettes.
Rebuilding, reconditioning, fabrication or
   restoration services.

592
Roett's Trophies
P.O. Box 10793
Daytona Beach, FL 32020

Awards and trophies for all purposes.
Free catalog.

593
Roger Brown
2413 Gunn Road
Carmichael, CA 95608

Parts and services.
1961-66 full-sized models (i.e., BelAirs, Biscaynes,
    Caprices, Impalas, station wagons and so on).

594
Roger DeFord
8201 East 9th Street
Buena Park, CA 90620

Cosmetic wood trim and interior body framing.

595
Roger D. Hunter
Route 2
Huntingburg, IN 47542

New, used, new-old-stock or reproduction parts and
    services.
All 1955-57 models, excluding Corvettes.

596
Roger Nevrel
P.O. Box 296
Sun Valley, CA 91352

New, used, new-old-stock or reproduction parts and
    services.
All 1955-57 models, excluding Corvettes.

597
Rollow Radio Repair
Route 3, Box 140
Jay, OK 74346

Sales and repair of new, new-old-stock,
    reproduction or rebuilt radios, speakers and
    boosters.

598
Ronnie Cochran
Route 1
Afton, TN 37616

Mechanical parts, accessories, body parts, interior
    parts, trim, chrome, electrical parts, hardware
    and other general parts.
All models, all years.

599
RPM
Box 3690
San Jose, CA 95156

New, used, new-old-stock, reproduction or rebuilt
    parts and services.
Corvettes, all years.
Free catalog.

600
R&R Classics
10014 Old Lincoln Trail
Fairview Heights, IL 62208

New, used, new-old-stock or reproduction parts and
    services.
All 1955–57 models, excluding Corvettes.

601
R&S Auto Parts
Department B
P.O. Box 101
Mendham, NJ 07945

Rechromed bumpers.

602
Russ Binder
14238 Friar Street
Van Nuys, CA 91401

New, used, new-old-stock, reproduction or rebuilt
parts and services.
Chevelles, El Caminos and Malibus from 1964 to
present.

603
Sander's Corvette Enterprises
5303 Valley Road
Fairfield, AL 35064

New, used, new-old-stock, reproduction or rebuilt
parts and services.
Corvettes, all years.
Location, purchasing, selling and trading of cars
and parts.
All models.

604
Sanders Reproduction Glass
P.O. Box 522
Hillsboro, OR 97123

New, new-old-stock or reproduction windows,
windshields and other glass parts.
All models and years.

605
San Diego Corvair Club
3052 Macaulay Street
San Diego, CA 92106

Restoration, preservation and collection.
Any model.

606
Seckman's Antique Car Radio and Speaker
Rebuilding
5340 Sandra Drive
Ravenna, OH 44266

Sales and repair of new, new-old-stock,
reproduction or rebuilt radios, speakers and
boosters.

607
Sermersheims Corvette Corner, Inc.
3817 North Saint Joseph Avenue
Evansville, IN 47712

New, used, new-old-stock, reproduction or rebuilt
parts and services.
Corvettes, all years.

608
Sherman and Associates
27940 Groesbeck
Department HR
Roseville, MI 48066

New, used, new-old-stock, reproduction or rebuilt
body and body trim parts.

609
Show Cars by Brad Ranweiler
Route 3, Box 9
New Ulm, MN 56073

Parts and services.
1958–66 full-sized models (i.e., BelAirs, Biscaynes,
Caprices, Impalas, station wagons and so on).
Mechanical parts, accessories, body parts, interior
parts, trim, chrome, electrical parts, hardware
and other general parts.

610
Sioux Plating Company, Inc.
428 East 9th
South Sioux City, NE 68776

Chrome, cadmium and silver plating; metal
polishing; and so on.

611
The 65–66 Full Size Chevy Club
126 Charles Road
Southampton, PA 18966

Restoration, preservation and collection.
Any model.

Parts and services.

1965–66 full-sized models (i.e., BelAirs, Biscaynes, Caprices, Impalas, station wagons and so on).

612
SK Classics
27 Lyman Street, Suite 603
Springfield, MA 01103

Location, purchasing, selling and trading of cars and parts.
All models.

613
Southwest Chevelle
3749 West Buchanan
Phoenix, AZ 85009

New, used, new-old-stock, reproduction or rebuilt parts and services.
Chevelles, El Caminos and Malibus from 1964 to present.
Send SASE for catalog.

614
Southwestern Classic Chevrolet
1230–B Dan Gould Drive
Arlington, TX 76017

New, used, new-old-stock, reproduction or rebuilt parts and services.
Camaros from 1967 to present; Chevelles, El Caminos and Malibus from 1964 to present.

615
The Speaker Shop
318 South Wahsatch Avenue
Colorado Springs, CO 80903

Sales and repair of new, new-old-stock, reproduction or rebuilt radios, speakers and boosters.

616
Specialized Investment Motor Company
P.O. Box 715
Napoleon, OH 43545

New, used, new-old-stock, reproduction or rebuilt
parts and services; location, purchasing, selling
and trading of cars and parts.
Corvettes, all years.

617
Specialty Chevy Products
1975 Northwest 92nd
Des Moines, IA 50322

Mechanical parts, accessories, body parts, interior
parts, trim, chrome, electrical parts, hardware
and other general parts.
All models, all years.

618
Speedomotive
12061 Slausen Avenue
Sante Fe Springs, CA 90670

New, used, new-old-stock, reproduction or rebuilt
engines, powerplant parts and so on.
Catalog, $4.00.

619
The Spindle People
4865 Warwick South
Department C
Canfield, OH 44406

New, used, new-old-stock, reproduction or rebuilt
suspension parts and services.
Corvettes, all years.

620
Springfield Auto Recyclers
P.O. Box 127
Springfield, OR 97477

Mechanical parts, accessories, body parts, interior
parts, trim, chrome, electrical parts, hardware
and other general parts.
All models, all years.
New, used, new-old-stock, reproduction or rebuilt
parts and services.
Pickups and trucks, all years.

621
Ssnake-Oyl Products
15775 North Hillcrest, Suite 508–541
Dallas, TX 75248

Fabric cleaning and treatment.
Free information.

622
Stainless Steel Brakes Corporation
11470 Main Road
Clarence, NY 14031

New, used, new-old-stock, reproduction or rebuilt
    brake parts.
Free catalog.

623
Standard Automotive
520 Payne Avenue
Saint Paul, MN 55101

New, used, new-old-stock, reproduction or rebuilt
    suspension parts and services.
Corvettes, all years.

624
Stans Chevelle Parts
74 Hadden Avenue West
West Berlin, NJ 08091

New, used, new-old-stock, reproduction or rebuilt
    parts and services.
Chevelles, El Caminos and Malibus from 1964 to
    present.

625
Steele Quality Reproduction Rubber
Department H–88
1601 Highway 150 East
Denver, NC 28037

New, new-old-stock or reproduction weather
    stripping, moldings, gaskets, seals and other
    rubber parts.
Catalog, $2.00.

626
Stelton Automotive
769 Fischer Boulevard
Department HMN
Tom's River, NJ 08753

Mechanical parts, accessories, body parts, interior
  parts, trim, chrome, electrical parts, hardware
  and other general parts.
All models, 1955–72.
Catalog, $5.00.

627
Sterling Corvette and Camaro
Route 1, Box 307F
Leesburg, VA 22075

New, used, new-old-stock, reproduction or rebuilt
  parts and services.
Corvettes, all years; Camaros from 1967 to present.

628
Steve Davis Enterprises
3909 Cashion Place
Oklahoma City, OK 73112

New, used, new-old-stock, reproduction or rebuilt
  parts and services; location, purchasing, selling
  and trading of vehicles and parts.
Pickups and trucks, all years.
Catalog, $2.00.

629
Steve Gregori
4017 East Huntington
Fresno, CA 93702

Power brake booster restoration.

630
Steve's Auto Restorations
5705 Northeast 105th, Unit G
Portland, OR 97220

Rebuilding, reconditioning, fabrication or
  restoration services.

138

631
Steve's Camaros
548 Kansas Street
Department CCB
San Francisco, CA 94107

New, used, new-old-stock, reproduction or rebuilt
   parts and services.
Camaros from 1967 to present.

632
Steve's Speedometer
Box 156
Agawam, MA 01001

Mechanical tachometer, speedometer and
   transducer repair.

633
Stoudt Auto Sales
Warren and Carbon Streets
Reading, PA 19601

New, used, new-old-stock, reproduction or rebuilt
   parts and services.
Corvettes, all years.

634
Street Machine Specialties
2538 Hennepin Avenue, F-688
Minneapolis, MN 55405

New, used, new-old-stock, reproduction or rebuilt
   high-performance parts and services.

635
Street Specialty
871 North Hanover
Department R118
Pottstown, PA 19464

Mechanical parts, accessories, body parts, interior
   parts, trim, chrome, electrical parts, hardware
   and other general parts.
All models, all years.

636
Strictly String Ray
2595 Ogden Avenue
Lisle, IL 60532

New, used, new-old-stock, reproduction or rebuilt
parts and services; location, purchasing, selling
and trading of cars and parts.
Corvettes, all years.

637
The Strip Shoppe, Inc.
1815 South Division Avenue
Orlando, FL 32805

Paint and rust stripping.

638
Sunshine State Classics
P.O. Box 14376
Orlando, FL 32857

Restoration, preservation and collection.
Any model.

639
Superior Parts
162 West Hills Road
Huntington Station, NY 11746

Mechanical parts, accessories, body parts, interior
parts, trim, chrome, electrical parts, hardware
and other general parts.
All models, all years.

640
Superior Stripping Company, Inc.
3020 Switzer Road
Columbus, OH 43219

Paint and rust stripping.

641
Super Sport Parts, Inc.
7138 Maddox Road
Lithonia, GA 30058

New, used, new-old-stock, reproduction or rebuilt
parts and services.

Camaros from 1967 to present; Chevelles, El
Caminos and Malibus from 1964 to present; full-
sized models (i.e., BelAirs, Biscaynes, Caprices,
Impalas, station wagons and so on); Monte Carlos
from 1970 to present; Novas and Chevy IIs from
1962 to present.

642

Sure-Vette Products
P.O. Box 10647
Napa, CA 94581

New, used, new-old-stock, reproduction or rebuilt
parts and services.
Corvettes, all years.

643

Surplus Supply Company
Box 9047
Akron, OH 44305

New, used, new-old-stock, reproduction or rebuilt
body and body trim parts.

644

Sussex Motor and Coach Works
P.O. Box 15
107 Avenue L
Matamoras, PA 18336

Rebuilding, reconditioning, fabrication or
restoration services.

645

SWAS
510 General Hodges SE
Albuquerque, NM 87123

Seatbelts and hardware.

646

Ted Williams Chevelle Parts
10838 Stockesberry Road
Lisbon, OH 44432

New, used, new-old-stock, reproduction or rebuilt
parts and services.

Chevelles, El Caminos and Malibus from 1964 to
present.

Catalog, $2.00.

647
TEMCO, Inc.
10913 I-76
Fort Morgan, CO 80701

Custom-built truck beds.

648
Terrill Machine, Inc.
Route 2, Box 61
De Leon, TX 76444

New, used, new-old-stock, reproduction or rebuilt
engines, powerplant parts and so on.

649
Theil Auto Enterprises
Route 1, Box 26
New London, WI 54961

New, used, new-old-stock, reproduction or rebuilt
body and body trim parts.

650
3B Innovations
P.O. Box 1033
Atascadero, CA 93423

New, used, new-old-stock, reproduction or rebuilt
body and body trim parts.

651
348/409 Connection
813 South Valley
New Ulm, MN 56073

New, used, new-old-stock, reproduction or rebuilt
348/409 engines, powerplant parts and so on.

652
Timothy Cox
1209 McClellan Way
Stockton, CA 95207

Custom firewall and kickboard insulators.

653
Tim Pilato
45 4th Street
Somerville, NJ 08876

New, used, new-old-stock or reproduction parts and
  services.
All 1955–57 models, excluding Corvettes.

654
Titles
P.O. Box 36904
Birmingham, AL 35236

Title location and securement companies.

655
Todd Murthum Reproductions
Box 652
Utica, MI 48087

Cosmetic wood trim and interior body framing.

656
Tom's Obsolete Chevy Parts
14 Delta Drive
Pawtucket, RI 02860

Mechanical parts, accessories, body parts, interior
  parts, trim, chrome, electrical parts, hardware
  and other general parts.
All models from 1955 to present.
Send SASE for catalog.

657
Tom's Truck Parts
525 15th Place SW
Miami, OK 74354

New, used, new-old-stock, reproduction or rebuilt
parts and services.
Pickups and trucks, all years.
Send SASE for catalog.

658
Tower Paint
Box 677
Oshkosh, WI 54902

Color-matched aerosol paints.

659
Tracy Performance
29069 Calahan
Roseville, MI 48066

New, used, new-old-stock, reproduction or rebuilt
parts and services.
Corvettes, all years.
New, used, new-old-stock, reproduction or rebuilt
engines, powerplant parts and so on.

660
Trans-Ocean Auto
Route 5
3 Lentine Drive
Flemington, NJ 08822

Automobile transportation.

661
Tri-Chevy Association
Route 1, Box 172
Elwood, IL 60421

Restoration, preservation and collection.
Any 1955–57 Chevrolet.

662
Trim Tags, Inc.
3631 Glenview Road
Glenview, IL 60025

Body and interior trim color-code tags.

144

663
Truck Carpet Company
310 New Orangeburg Road
Lexington, SC 29072

Interior fabric, hardware and trim.

664
Truck Shop
424 West Chapman Avenue
Orange, CA 92666

New, used, new-old-stock, reproduction or rebuilt
    parts and services.
Pickups and trucks, all years.
Free catalog.

665
The Truck Shop
604 West Avenue North
Crossville, TN 38555

New, used, new-old-stock, reproduction or rebuilt
    parts and services.
Pickups and trucks, all years.
Free price list.

666
Truck Stop
4402 Highway 173
Caledonia, IL 61001

New, used, new-old-stock, reproduction or rebuilt
    parts and services.
Pickups and trucks, all years.

667
Tulsa Dry-Strip
4748 South 101st East Avenue
Tulsa, OK 74145

Dry paint and rust stripping.

668
Unique Antiques
Route 3, Box 25
Fort McCoy, FL 32637

New, used, new-old-stock or reproduction parts and
    services.
All 1911–54 models of cars and trucks, excluding
    Corvettes.
Mechanical parts, accessories, body parts, interior
    parts, trim, chrome, electrical parts, hardware
    and other general parts.
All models.

669
United States Camaro Club
1654 Mardon Drive
Dayton, OH 45432

Restoration, preservation and collection.
Any model.

670
Urethane Concepts
P.O. Box 14706
Phoenix, AZ 85063

Urethane body and body trim parts.

671
USA–1 Interiors
Route 322, P.O. Box 691
Department HM
Williamstown, NJ 08094

Interior fabric, hardware and trim.

672
US Body Source
320 Paint Street
Catalog #5
Rockledge, FL 39955

New, new-old-stock or reproduction body and body
    trim parts.
New, used, new-old-stock, reproduction or rebuilt

146

parts and services.
Pickups and trucks, all years.
Catalog, $1.00.

673
US Muscle Camaro Parts
P.O. Box 372
Department BG
Finksburg, MD 21048

New, used, new-old-stock, reproduction or rebuilt
parts and services.
Camaros from 1967 to present.

674
Valley Forge Restorations
P.O. Box 1133
Apache Junction, AZ 85217

Rebuilding, reconditioning, fabrication or
restoration services.

675
Valley Vinyl Service
609 Bird Avenue
San Jose, CA 95125

Interior fabric, hardware and trim.

676
Van Nuys Antique Radio
13133 Weddington Street
Van Nuys, CA 91401

Sales and repair of new, new-old-stock,
reproduction or rebuilt radios, speakers and
boosters.

677
Van Steel
1141-A Court Street
Clearwater, FL 34616

Mechanical parts, accessories, body parts, interior
parts, trim, chrome, electrical parts, hardware
and other general parts; rebuilding,
reconditioning, fabrication or restoration services.
All models, all years.

678
Vette Products
7490 30th Avenue North
Department CC 3–8
Saint Petersburg, FL 33710

New, used, new-old-stock, reproduction or rebuilt
  parts and services.
Corvettes, all years.

679
Vette Products of Michigan
2330 West Clarkston Road
Lake Orion, MI 48035

New, used, new-old-stock, reproduction or rebuilt
  parts and services.
Corvettes, all years.

680
Vette Sette
212 7th Street SW
New Philadelphia, OH 44663

New, used, new-old-stock, reproduction or rebuilt
  brake parts.
Corvettes.

681
Vettes 'n' Stuff
Route 2, Box 20
Danville, IL 61832

New, used, new-old-stock, reproduction or rebuilt
  parts and services.
Corvettes, all years.

682
Vintage Auto Parts
24300 Highway 9
Woodinville, WA 98072

New, used, new-old-stock or reproduction parts and
  services.
All 1911–54 models of cars and trucks, excluding
  Corvettes.

Mechanical parts, accessories, body parts, interior
parts, trim, chrome, electrical parts, hardware
and other parts.
All models.

683
Vintage Chevrolet Club of America
P.O. Box 5387
Orange, CA 92667

Restoration, preservation and collection.
Any model.

684
Vintage Tin Auto Parts
4550-A Scotty Lane
Hutchinson, KS 67502

Mechanical parts, accessories, body parts, interior
parts, trim, chrome, electrical parts, hardware
and other general parts.
All models, all years.

685
Vintage Vette Clock and Gauge
14831 Honor Court
Woodbridge, VA 22193

Sales and repair of new, used, new-old-stock,
reproduction or rebuilt clocks and gauges.

686
Virginia Vettes
110 Maid Marion Place
Williamsburg, VA 23185

New, used, new-old-stock, reproduction or rebuilt
parts and services.
Corvettes, all years.

687
Volo Antique Auto Museum
27640 West Highway 120
Volo, IL 60073

Location, purchasing, selling and trading of cars
and parts.
All models.

688
Volunteer State Chevy Parts
Drawer D
Highway 41 South
Greenbrier, TN 37073

Mechanical parts, accessories, body parts, interior
    parts, trim, chrome, electrical parts, hardware
    and other general parts.
All models, all years.

689
Volunteer Vette Products
P.O. Box 9474
Knoxville, TN 37940

New, used, new-old-stock, reproduction or rebuilt
    parts and services.
Corvettes, all years.
Free catalog.

690
Von Reece Auctioneers
4400 Bunny Run
Austin, TX 78746

Classic and antique auto auction services.
Free brochure.

691
VVR
2101 South Street
Sacramento, CA 95816

Mechanical parts, accessories, body parts, interior
    parts, trim, chrome, electrical parts, hardware
    and other general parts.
All models, all years.
Send SASE for catalog.

692
Wacha's
1208 South 7th Avenue
Marshalltown, IA 50158

Mechanical parts, accessories, body parts, interior parts, trim, chrome, electrical parts, hardware and other general parts.
All models, all years.
Free catalog.

693
Wade's
12512 Northeast 4th Plain
Vancouver, WA 98682

New, used, new-old-stock, reproduction or rebuilt parts and services.
Chevelles, El Caminos and Malibus from 1964 to present.

694
Walee Carbs
680 Prospect Street
Chicopee, MA 01020

New, new-old-stock, reproduction or rebuilt fuel system parts and services.

695
Wally Motors
1345 North Fitzgerald, Unit B
Rialto, CA 92376

New, used, new-old-stock or reproduction parts and services.
All 1955-57 models, excluding Corvettes.
Send SASE and specify needs.

696
Walter Miller
6710 Brooklawn Parkway
Syracuse, NY 13211

Manuals, parts books, price books, catalogs and other literature.
Send SASE for catalog.

697
Walter's Engineering
7252 Southwest 55 Avenue
Miami, FL 33143

Hardware.
Corvettes.
Catalog, $2.00.

698
Walter Truck and Parts Locator
203 Towle Road
Chester, NH 03036

Location, purchasing, selling and trading of vehicles
    and parts.
Pickups and trucks, all models.

699
Waseca Glass and Mirror
707 South State Street
Waseca, MN 56093

New, new-old-stock or reproduction windows,
    windshields and other glass parts.
All models and years.

700
Weinstein
44 Valley Brook #HMN
East Amherst, NY 14051

Interior fabric, hardware and trim.
Send SASE for catalog.

701
West Coast Porcelain
9868 Kale Street
South El Monte, CA 91733

Chrome, cadmium and silver plating; metal
    polishing; and so on.

702
Western Corvette Supply
P.O. Box 307
Bothell, WA 98041

New, used, new-old-stock, reproduction or rebuilt
parts and services.
Corvettes, all years.
Interior fabric, hardware and trim.

703
Wheel Repair Service of New England
Department H
317 Southbridge Street
Auburn, MA 01501

Wheels and wheel accessories; rebuilding,
reconditioning, fabrication or restoration services.
All models.
Catalog, $2.00.

704
Whip-n-Ride Auto Sales
305 East Highway 20
Gordon, NE 69343

Location, purchasing, selling and trading of cars
and parts.
All models.

705
Wholesale Express
120 East Plymouth Street
Bremen, IN 46506

Mechanical parts, accessories, body parts, interior
parts, trim, chrome, electrical parts, hardware
and other general parts; new, used, new-old-
stock, reproduction or rebuilt high-performance
parts and services.
All models, all years.

706
Willcox Chevrolet
2005 Highway 62
Jeffersonville, IN 47130

GM dealers.
Restoration and preservation services; new, new-
old-stock, reproduction and rebuilt parts and

services; mechanical parts, accessories, body parts, interior parts, trim, chrome, electrical parts, hardware and other general parts.
All models, all years.

707

Williamson's Instrument Service
Highway 282
Chester, AR 72934

Sales and repair of new, used, new-old-stock, reproduction or rebuilt clocks and gauges.

708

Williams Shop Equipment
Rural Route
Wheatridge, CO 80033

Special tools and machinery for restoration and preservation.

709

Willie's Antique Tires
5257 West Diversey Avenue
Chicago, IL 60639

New, new-old-stock or reproduction antique and classic tires.

710

Wilson's Classic Auto
Route 1, Box 150
Congerville, IL 61729

New, used, new-old-stock, reproduction or rebuilt parts and services.
Corvettes, all years.

711

Wilsons Quality Trailers
1008 East Walnut
Sioux Falls, SD 57103

Transport trailers and parts.

712
Window Treatment Center
1412 West 12th Street
Sioux Falls, SD 57104

Shading and ornamental window treatment.

713
Winona-Van Norman
4730 West Highway 61
Winona, MN 55987

Special tools and machinery for restoration and
    preservation.

714
The Woodgraining Department
720 Del Rey
Modesto, CA 75350

Cosmetic wood trim and interior body framing.

715
Woodworks, Limited
Route 1
Mechanicsburg, IL 62545

Cosmetic wood trim and interior body framing.

716
W. Strobl
55769 Washington
Rochester, MI 48064

New, used, new-old-stock, reproduction or rebuilt
    parts and services.
Convertibles, all years.
Send SASE for catalog.

717
WW Motor Cars and Parts, Inc.
P.O. Box 667
132 Main Street
Broadway, VA 22815

Mechanical parts, accessories, body parts, interior
    parts, trim, chrome, electrical parts, hardware

and other general parts.
All models, all years.

718
Year One, Inc
Box 450131
Group HMN8
Atlanta, GA 30345

New, used, new-old-stock, reproduction or rebuilt
parts and services.
Camaros from 1967 to present; Chevelles, El
Caminos and Malibus from 1964 to present.
Catalog, $2.00; specify model.

719
Yother
16848 Alisal Court
San Lorenzo, CA 94580

Special tools and machinery for restoration and
preservation.

720
Zigmont Billus
Route 1, East River Road
Fort Edward, NY 12828

Rebabbitting.

721
ZIP Products
5501 Mechanicsville Pike
Mechanicsville, VA 23111

Cooling and fuel system plumbing, built to factory
specifications.

722
Z&Z Auto
233 North Lemon
Orange, CA 92666

New, used, new-old-stock, reproduction or rebuilt
parts and services.
Camaros from 1967 to present.

Index

Accessories (cosmetic and mechanical): 82, 90, 144, 167, 182, 295, 297, 309, 381, 384, 445, 543.

Appraisals and estimates: 5, 38, 49, 197, 376.

Body and body trim parts: 3, 6, 17, 31, 44, 51, 69, 77, 90, 114, 148, 218, 235, 254, 265, 291, 293, 294, 310, 378, 398, 408, 432, 435, 452, 466, 502, 509, 513, 523, 601, 608, 637, 640, 643, 649, 655, 658, 662, 667, 670, 672, 715.

Brake parts: 54, 208, 271, 276, 284, 300, 379, 414, 481, 515, 552, 622, 629, 680.

Brokers (location, purchasing, selling and trading of vehicles and parts): 64, 89, 109, 110, 158, 166, 179, 180, 222, 224, 254, 273, 281, 347, 350, 368, 397, 438, 456, 457, 491, 570, 603, 612, 616, 628, 636, 687, 690, 698, 704.

Camaros from 1967 to present, parts and services: 2, 13, 26, 33, 42, 62, 79, 98, 99, 100, 102, 113, 114, 117, 140, 155, 175, 245, 267, 298, 300, 314, 391, 444, 465, 489, 527, 528, 536, 576, 614, 627, 631, 641, 673, 722.

Chevelle, El Camino and Malibu parts and services: 21, 33, 40, 65, 79, 80, 93, 114, 116, 125, 126, 127, 128, 130, 134, 150, 168, 225, 227, 229, 256, 259, 267, 272, 279, 314, 375, 399, 404, 442, 527, 528, 602, 613, 614, 624, 641, 646, 693, 718.

Clocks and gauges: 174, 194, 195, 205, 236, 247, 255, 258, 363, 395, 407, 458, 468, 496, 530, 575, 632, 685, 707.

Clubs involved with restoration, preservation and collection: 1, 101, 120, 136, 149, 161, 212, 301, 329, 366, 422, 431, 433, 470, 482, 483, 484, 485, 486, 487, 488, 497, 498, 504, 605, 611, 638, 661, 669, 683.

Convertible parts and services: 183, 184, 343, 357, 380, 462, 503, 716.

Cooling system parts and services: 35, 67, 95, 121, 160, 238, 248, 425, 551, 561, 580.

Corvair parts and services: 23, 66, 151, 185, 186, 187, 430.

Corvette parts and services: 16, 25, 59, 72, 76, 82, 89, 104, 105, 134, 141, 176, 188, 189, 190, 191, 192, 193, 194, 196, 197, 198, 199, 200, 201, 202, 203, 204, 205, 206, 207, 208, 209, 210, 214, 222, 234, 246, 252, 253, 254, 271, 272, 274, 275, 281, 300, 317, 322, 331, 333, 344, 347, 359, 367, 388, 390, 402, 403, 416, 428, 435, 438, 439, 441, 443, 454, 493, 525, 532, 548, 581, 582, 599, 603, 607, 616, 619, 623, 627, 633, 636, 642, 678, 679, 680, 681, 685, 686, 689, 697, 702, 710.

Electrical system parts and services: 243, 285, 315, 316, 339, 344, 455, 472, 492, 496, 500, 544, 567, 573, 577, 585.

Engines, parts and so on: 9, 27, 47, 54, 58, 60, 103, 144, 145, 241, 276, 278, 283, 286, 287, 288, 289, 313, 337, 342, 346, 370, 379, 414, 471, 477, 534, 539, 554, 574, 590, 618, 720.

Exhaust parts or complete systems: 8, 78, 93, 96, 257, 400.

Fuel system parts and services: 35, 74, 106, 107, 108, 141, 143, 146, 371, 386, 461, 496, 500, 559, 580, 694.

Full-sized models (i.e., BelAirs, Biscaynes, Caprices, Impalas, station wagons and so on), parts and services: 23, 114, 145, 296, 355, 421, 556, 586, 593, 609, 611, 641.

General parts (mechanical parts, accessories, body parts, interior parts, trim, chrome, electrical parts, hardware and so on): 3, 14, 23, 28, 43, 46, 50, 71, 75, 86, 111, 112, 118, 124, 132, 137, 139, 152, 158, 159, 164, 223, 244, 250, 260, 270, 297, 303, 305, 324, 338, 340, 348, 355, 381, 383, 385, 392, 398, 413, 414, 448, 450, 454, 460, 463, 464, 478, 479, 480, 499, 505, 506, 507, 510, 513, 520, 529, 531, 537, 547, 553, 554, 565, 568, 571, 572, 579, 587, 598, 609, 617, 620, 626, 635, 639, 656, 677, 684, 688, 691, 692, 705, 706.

Glass (windows, windshields and so on): 163, 321, 369, 394, 412, 509, 546, 604, 699, 712.

GM dealers: 348, 428, 706.

Hardware (trim sources, bolts, fasteners and miscellaneous hardware): 45, 171, 323.

High-performance parts and services: 19, 55, 76, 81, 226, 288, 295, 297, 358, 541, 560, 634, 705.

Insurance: 15, 181.

Interior fabric, hardware and trim: 7, 24, 26, 36, 68, 73, 94, 114, 129, 147, 168, 202, 218, 230, 248, 264, 282, 290, 334, 335, 360, 364, 365, 400, 435, 436, 501, 521, 566, 621, 645, 655, 663, 675, 700, 715.

Literature (manuals, parts books, price books, catalogs and so on): 4, 32, 46, 48, 50, 138, 165, 172, 249, 263, 292, 306, 308, 417, 419, 437, 535, 578, 696.

Miscellaneous: 153, 182, 238, 243, 269, 282, 313, 335, 384, 389, 423, 451, 475, 542, 592, 652, 658, 662, 670, 721.

Monte Carlo parts and services, 1970 to present: 33, 114, 116, 375, 404, 527, 528, 641.

1911-54 cars and trucks, excluding Corvettes; parts and services: 11, 23, 28, 87, 131, 135, 232, 294, 297, 327, 332, 377, 415, 440, 469, 512, 522, 524, 526, 556, 668, 682.

1955-57 models, excluding Corvettes; parts and services: 23, 39, 173, 213, 227, 259, 262, 266, 320, 355, 396, 434, 459, 474, 495, 505, 520, 556, 591, 595, 596, 600, 653, 695.

Nova and Chevy parts and services, 1962 to present: 33, 114, 119, 245, 393, 411, 467, 527, 528, 641.

Pickup and truck parts and services: 61, 88, 91, 133, 229, 233, 237, 242, 251, 261, 294, 297, 309, 319, 325, 341, 353, 387, 445, 507, 517, 519, 568, 588, 620, 628, 647, 657, 663, 664, 665, 666, 672.

Plating and metal working (chrome, cadmium and silver plating; metal polishing; and so on): 83, 142, 215, 219, 280, 307, 310, 312, 328, 336, 354, 426, 447, 473, 533, 538, 540, 549, 550, 557, 558, 569, 601, 610, 701.

Radios, speakers and boosters: 29, 34, 97, 122, 216, 217, 228, 311, 318, 372, 449, 562, 563, 597, 606, 615, 676.

Rebuilding, reconditioning, fabrication or restoration services: 12, 20, 21, 30, 35, 37, 52, 53, 56, 63, 77, 81, 84, 85, 143, 154, 156, 162, 169, 193, 206, 209, 252, 254, 270, 277, 282, 284, 304, 330, 340, 343, 345, 346, 347, 349, 359, 360, 361, 373, 374, 390, 397, 405, 424, 443, 446, 496, 500, 509, 515, 518, 582, 583, 591, 594, 603, 630, 636, 637, 640, 644, 667, 674, 677, 703, 710, 714.

Restoration and preservation tools and machinery: 34, 220, 351, 362, 420, 555, 589, 708, 713, 719.

Rubber parts (weather stripping, moldings, gaskets, seals and so on): 22, 157, 168, 170, 201, 453, 513, 625.

Suspension parts, supplies and services: 30, 54, 57, 177, 221, 235, 276, 278, 299, 379, 382, 410, 414, 418, 476, 490, 515, 619.

Tires, antique and classic: 178, 709.

Title location and securement: 123, 654.

Trailers and parts: 268, 584, 711.

Transmissions or parts: 10, 231, 240, 302, 313, 401, 429, 502, 511, 545.

Transportation services: 239, 304, 326, 352, 427, 494, 660.

Wheels and wheel accessories: 3, 18, 234, 353, 356, 562, 703.